FEEDING THE FUTURE

FEEDING THE FUTURE

The Emergence of School Lunch Programs as Global Social Policy

JENNIFER GEIST RUTLEDGE

RUTGERS UNIVERSITY PRESS

New Brunswick, New Jersey, and London

10-18-16
LN
$27.95

Library of Congress Cataloging-in-Publication Data
Names: Rutledge, Jennifer Geist.
Title: Feeding the future : the emergence of school lunch programs as global social policy / Jennifer Geist Rutledge.
Description: New Brunswick, New Jersey : Rutgers University Press, [2016] | Includes bibliographical references and index.
Identifiers: LCCN 2015028637| ISBN 9780813573328 (hardcover : alk. paper) | ISBN 9780813573311 (pbk. : alk. paper) | ISBN 9780813573335 (e-book (epub) : alk. paper) | ISBN 9780813573342 (e-book (web pdf) : alk. paper)
Subjects: LCSH: School children—Food. | School children—Nutrition. | School lunchrooms, cafeterias, etc.
Classification: LCC LB3475 .R88 2016 | DDC 371.7/16—dc23
LC record available at http://lccn.loc.gov/2015028637

A British Cataloging-in-Publication record for this book is available from the British Library.

Visit our website: http://rutgerspress.rutgers.edu

Manufactured in the United States of America

For my mother, Gretel Geist Rutledge (1941–2015)

CONTENTS

ACKNOWLEDGMENTS

In the fall of 2005, I took a class called Family, Children, and the State with Daniel Kelliher at the University of Minnesota. This class, unusual in its focus for a political science PhD program, took seriously the overlap between families and the state and challenged us to consider the ways in which the state intervenes in and directly creates families. As an ardent gardener, I had become interested in school gardens, which were popping up all over Minneapolis and seemed like an easy solution to the problems of unappetizing school meals and obesity. In my seminar paper for that class, I explored the nascent efforts to challenge and transform the United States' school lunch program. That paper was the seed of this book, as it focused my interests on how food policy can work as social policy, as well as the way in which families and states negotiate over the care of children.

Thus this project started, as so many first books do, as my dissertation. The book looks substantially different than the dissertation, having benefitted from several years away from the topic, an entire rethinking of the theory, a new focus on regional variation, and further field research. However, I wouldn't have made it to the book if I hadn't started with the dissertation, and as such I must thank Kathryn Sikkink, who shepherded that project. In addition, Sally Kenney and Ben Ansell were extremely encouraging and provided advice and assistance as I began to turn it into a book.

I was embraced by my colleagues at John Jay College and thank several of them for reading different versions of these chapters. In particular Susan Kang, Veronica Michel, Jack Jacobs, and Josh Wilson provided extremely helpful feedback on different parts of the book. Samantha Majic proved to be an extraordinary friend and critic and read and reread most of these pages.

Thanks are owed to Jane Bowers, provost at John Jay College, who funded my research trip to India, as well as the PSC-CUNY, which funded my research in Norway. During both trips, I was welcomed into the offices, homes, and schools of numerous people, all of whom helped shape my understanding of their countries' histories, as well as the centrality of school meals to hunger reduction, education, culture, and family. This book would not exist in its present form without the many conversations I had on these two trips.

Of course, there is no book without a publisher, and Peter Mickulas saw promise in this project from the beginning. The reviewers he found were incredibly insightful and generous, and the book is much better because of them. I thank them and Peter for this. Parts of chapter 3 on the United Kingdom and chapter 4 on the United States previously appeared in *History of Education*, while the Norway case in chapter 3 was presented in much more detail in an article in *Food, Culture, and Society*. Both sections of the book are immeasurably better due to the anonymous reviewers for these two journals.

My wife, Autumn, read far more of this book than she ever wanted and did so with grace and a good eye for detail. I can never thank her enough for her support. Perhaps, though, the greatest thanks is owed to my mother. While initially surprised by the subject, she quickly became an enthusiastic supporter and even accompanied me on my research trips to Italy and India. In fact, in India she was quite the assistant, as many of my interviewees gravitated to this jolly, fleece-wearing lady, and she helped inject an ease into the conversations that might not otherwise have existed. She was diagnosed with terminal cancer one month after I received the book contract from Rutgers. I spent part of that fall sitting in hospital rooms with her, reading my revisions aloud to her, partly as an editing tool and partly as a diversion from the medical reality she was facing. If she was awake, she was a patient listener, although I think she wanted more fun stories and a little less social science. She passed away before the book was published. I am so grateful for her love.

FEEDING THE FUTURE

1 · INTRODUCTION

Today children in 151 countries receive free or subsidized school lunches. Yet just a hundred years ago, only a few local charities in a few European cities fed children. In other words, a program type that once was an occasional charity project exists today around the world as a common social benefits program. In particular, school lunch programs in developing countries are increasingly used as the primary method to address child malnutrition and encourage school attendance. Indeed, while other social benefits programs are under attack in both developed and developing countries, school lunch programs are well funded and have strong political support. This book's question is one of social policy formation: how and why did school lunch programs emerge? Given that all countries developed education systems, why do some countries have these programs and others do not? Further, what explains the lasting prevalence of these programs?

The development of school lunch programs is a surprise when one considers the relative lack of social policy focused on children and the lack of attention usually paid to chronic malnutrition. The twentieth century charted new types of intervention by states and other organizations into the lives of families with the creation of the welfare state. However, with the exception of compulsory education systems, children over five were left out of the nascent welfare states. Paternalist welfare states were largely concerned with the problems of the working man, and those child benefits that did develop were designed to compensate workers for the cost of their child; other states were maternalist welfare states and focused on the needs of mothers and infants (Skocpol 1992). In both paternalist and maternalist welfare states, aside from the creation of educational systems, the needs of school-age children, particularly their physical needs, were generally left out of early welfare schemes.

The development of feeding programs for school children is also surprising due to the low level of interest malnutrition receives in the policy arena. A lack of attention to chronic hunger has historically been considered a principle characteristic of the international food regime (Hopkins and Puchala 1978, 25). The international food aid system is programmed and targeted at emergency food shortages such as famines, rather than at chronic malnutrition. Within many countries, despite an almost universal desire for agricultural self-sufficiency, chronic malnutrition also endures. The slow process of building the necessary institutions, legal reforms, and asset redistribution systems to combat chronic malnutrition is certainly one of the causes for its endurance (Dreze and Sen 1989, 8). The structural causes of endemic malnutrition are so great and so deep that many countries have had difficulties addressing them. However, as argued throughout this book, the creation of school lunch programs was only partially driven by a concern with reducing hunger and malnutrition.

Despite the difficulties inherent in creating policy to target malnutrition and the low level of practical attention children's issues have historically received, school lunch programs have emerged over the last hundred years in an effort to achieve a number of policy goals including, for instance, balancing agricultural surpluses, improving a country's development prospects, reducing malnutrition, and/or improving national security. School lunches have become an important part of the welfare state across the globe due to a combination of material and ideational factors, and now 368 million children receive school lunches in 151 countries. Specifically, states' choices about supporting national agriculture interacted with a variety of ideas in different national and international contexts to create a program type that has taken hold around the world in three distinct phases.

These phases can be seen in figures 1.1 and 1.2, which indicate when school lunch programs were created for the first time by any organization, such as a national government, an international organization, or a nongovernmental organization (figure 1.1), and when national governments first created school lunch programs (figure 1.2).

In the first phase, during the 1930s and 1940s, school lunches were created in a handful of South American and European countries and the United States. In South America, lunch programs were created in large cities in the

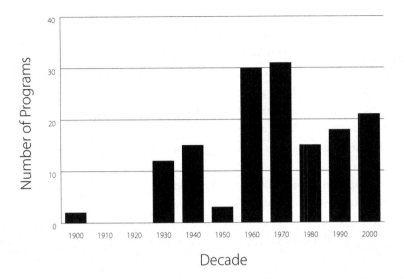

FIGURE 1.1. Number of School Lunch Programs by Decade, All
Sources: See the appendix.

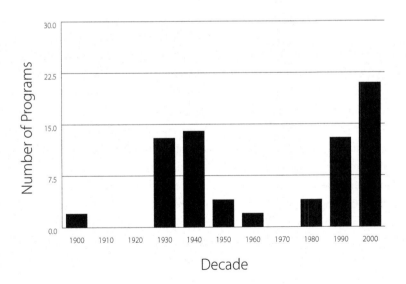

FIGURE 1.2. Programs Initiated by Own Government, by Decade
Sources: See the appendix.

former Spanish colonies, largely in response to labor's demands for aid during the Great Depression. In many ways, the development of these programs can be explained by theories that explain welfare state development as a product of worker power and leftist governments (Esping-Anderson 1990; Huber and Stephens 2001; Korpi 1989). This is unlike school lunch programs in most of the rest of the world, particularly Europe and the United States, where these conventional theories cannot explain the creation of their programs. It is the puzzle of these countries around which the book centers.

In Europe and the United States, child advocates and educational reformers, who had been documenting a connection between nutrition and educational abilities for years (*Lancet* 1883) and in many cases providing meals through the work of voluntary organizations, laid the groundwork for program emergence. However, they were not successful until they were able to link concerns with child hunger to other issues, such as normative frameworks about the role of women, concerns with national security, and ideas about welfare.

In the second phase, cognitive paradigms that specified a link between education and national development dominated policy making as school lunches were created as one of the foundational policies of the U.N.'s World Food Programme (WFP) during the 1960s and 1970s, which the U.N. then spread around the world. In the third phase, beginning in the 1990s, the cognitive paradigm of post-neoliberal economics motivated decision makers to switch to market-based solutions to child hunger. In this phase, the WFP began phasing out its school lunch programs in a number of countries; many countries chose to keep providing school meal programs while others chose to switch to a new way of providing aid through conditional cash transfer programs. Taking these differences into consideration, this study seeks to explain the differences across space and time in the creation of these programs.

The emergence of lunch programs can be understood largely as an unintended effect of agricultural policy that rewarded farmers for producing surpluses. Using John Kingdon's framework for policy emergence (2003), the policy problem was not malnourished children but rather agricultural surplus. School lunches provided a ready outlet for agricultural surplus, both during the period when they were first institutionalized as national policy in a handful of European states and the United States and when they were spread around the world through the U.N.'s World Food Programme. While different factors influenced policy adoption during each of these two waves of program emergence, the various adopting countries and the WFP shared the common factor of possessing agricultural surpluses. In the European states that created programs, almost all of them used price supports for agriculture that produced surpluses, while the WFP's activities were largely driven by U.S. agricultural policy and the attendant surpluses that were given to the WFP.

However, in each of the two waves of program emergence the decision, or policy solution, that funneling these surpluses into child feeding programs was best depended on different factors. In each of the cases of school lunch creation, policy entrepreneurs, motivated by a commitment to alleviate childhood malnutrition, harnessed ideas that were relevant to their state or organization in order to funnel agricultural surpluses into school lunch programs. While agricultural surpluses are a necessary condition for the creation of school lunch programs, they were not created until actors concerned with child malnutrition framed school lunches as a policy solution to other ideational factors, including national security and status, the role of women, and market economic theory, to list just a few. In short, material forces create a basic set of possibilities or parameters for policy, but actors, driven by an array of ideas, are the ones who figure out how to make use of these possibilities.

Importantly, the strength of each explanation, material or ideational, differs at the domestic/national level versus the global. The relative explanatory weight of ideas is much stronger at the domestic/national level than at the global level, where material interests predominate. At the global level, particularly in the case of the WFP, ideas are used to support an argument that the creation of school lunch programs is desirable and necessary, while program creation is driven by U.S. agricultural policy goals. At the domestic/national level, the strength of an ideational explanation varies by country, but for the most part ideas have a strong explanatory weight, in part because the creation of these programs was an innovation. Exploring the balance between these two factors and the difference between their relative explanatory values at different scales is one of the key contributions of this project.

IDEAS AND INTERESTS

How and why did school lunch programs emerge as social policy on a global level? This question falls squarely into the study of comparative and global social policy. Based in Marxist or Weberian thought, the study of social policy originally focused largely on material or institutional interests as the driving force behind policy creation (Campbell 1998, 379). Certainly a materialist explanation, which sees school lunches as a means to address the problem of agricultural surpluses, is key to understanding the prevalence of these programs. However, one cannot understand the emergence of these programs without also appreciating the role of ideas. Material forces, in this case agricultural surpluses, created the possibility for school lunches, as these food supplies could be funneled into lunch programs, but actors, driven by ideas, had to figure out how to make use of these materials. There are a variety of decisions governments could make in regards to food surpluses, including selling them on the open market, stockpiling them for the future, or donating them to other countries, all of which countries did and do. Thus, it took concerted political action and an explicit linking of various ideas to agriculture to produce school lunch programs.

It is the interaction of material and ideational factors that explains the emergence of school lunch programs as global social policy. In particular, those countries that prioritized agricultural policies that were more likely to produce surpluses tended to create school lunch programs, as these programs provide outlets for that surplus. However, there is a marked difference between the first phase of program emergence and the second phase when the World Food Programme adopted and spread school lunch programs. In the first phase, ideas played a strong role in the creation of the programs. Policy entrepreneurs who had been concerned about child malnutrition were able to step into the window of opportunity provided by the Great Depression and World War II and connect the material reality of agricultural surplus with these ideas: gender ideologies related to women's employment, concerns about national security, ideas about the role of the state in protecting the welfare of its citizens, and ideas about the goals of education interacted with these agricultural policies in different ways in different countries to produce school lunch programs. In the second phase, the strength of U.S. support for the World Food Programme, driven primarily by material concerns with agricultural subsidies and the attendant surpluses, were bolstered by new ideas about children as vital for national development to create school lunches as one of the few policy types that the WFP has consistently supported. In the third phase, ideas about economics and the role of the state fostered a change in school feeding that focuses on a public-private model of provision and, in some cases, the discontinuation of the programs themselves.

This argument builds on a long tradition of work on the role of ideas and interests in the policy-making process. In many ways, policy theory begins with Max Weber's contention that "not ideas, but material and ideal interests, directly govern men's conduct. Yet very frequently, the 'world images' that have been created by 'ideas' have, like switchmen, determined the tracks along which action has been pushed by the dynamic of interest" (Weber 1946, 280). This passage has traditionally been understood to highlight material self-interest as the driving force behind human action and government policy. In line with this understanding of the role of interests in policy making, conventional arguments about the policy-making process have been based in materialist explanations that focus on variables such as power, interests, and institutions (Bleich 2002, 1055; see also Evans, Rueschemeyer, and Skocpol 1985; Korpi 1983; Stevens 1979; Thelen 1999).

The standard explanation of Weber suggests that he believed that ideas can be reduced to interests, and matter only in that they provide the different tracks toward which interests push action (Bendix 1977; Blau 1996; Weber 1946). However, a contextual reading of Weber's famous passage suggests a much larger role for ideas and even that Weber understood interests to themselves be culturally constructed (Eastwood 2005, 90). When placed in context, the passage, which is largely about the concept of redemption, reveals equal analytic weight to material and ideal interests (Eastwood 2005, 92), and highlights the difference between ideas and ideal interests. For Weber, ideal interests can be understood as normative ends toward which one strives, while ideas can be understood as descriptions of the world and can include scientific theories or other "facts" about the world. This careful distinction between the terms ideas, ideal interests, and material interests means that in fact, ideas, and interests are inseparable, as it is only through ideas that interests have any meaning (T. Lewis 2007). This rereading suggests the need to analyze systematically the relationship between ideas and interests.

While a materialist interpretation of Weber long held sway for policy scholars, Hugh Heclo began exploring the interplay of ideas and interests in the creation of social policy through his idea of puzzling and powering (1974, 305). He argued that policy has often been driven more by the process of puzzling, or knowing and deciding, than that of powering, or of pure material interests. Heclo argued that social policy in Britain and Sweden can be primarily understood through a social learning perspective that emphasizes the role of ideas in helping policy makers, including civil servants, policy middlemen, and experts, diagnose problems and search for solutions through the "collective puzzlement on society's behalf" (1974, 305). It is only after puzzling has occurred that powering comes into play as political power is brought to press for particular solutions. Heclo's work brought a consideration of the role of ideas and learning more forcefully into our examinations of social policy.

Others have since begun to analyze the role of ideas in the policy process (see, for instance, Beland 2005; Berman 1998; Boli and Thomas 1999; Campbell 2002; Finnemore 1996; Sikikink 1991). For instance, marginal groups can have an influence on public policy making because of the strength of their ideas (Bleich 2002, 1055); very few public policy "problems" were problems until they were interpreted as such by policy makers or politicians (Stone 1989, 282). In the early 1990s, scholars began to consider how ideas could affect policy making, and some of the first work analyzed the conditions under which ideas might matter (Goldstein and Keohnane 1993; McDonough 1997). As the 1990s progressed, scholars began to consider how ideas and interests might interact (Risse-Kappen, Roop, and Sikkink 1999; Suchman 1997); Margaret Keck and Kathryn Sikkink's work on transnational advocacy networks (1998) illustrates this approach as they demonstrated that actors with principled ideas and beliefs use networks strategically to create new issues and to persuade, pressure, and gain leverage over much more powerful organizations and states. Indeed, considering the ways in which ideas and material factors interact is one of the more fruitful approaches to the study of policy making, as it moves beyond a static debate between material and idealist notions of policy making.

Ideas are an integral part of the policy-making process as they both create the institutional conditions that allow for the recognition of particular problems, as well as help actors navigate through those challenges. However, it is not enough to know that ideas are causal: it is also necessary to consider the different types of ideas and the ways in which these different types are likely to have effects on policy-making. There are a variety of idea types that influence the creation of policy, including cognitive paradigms, which can be understood as the "taken-for-granted world views . . . that specify cause and effect relationships" (Campbell 2002, 22), and normative frameworks, which are the "taken-for-granted assumptions about values, attitudes, [and] ideas" (Campbell 2002, 23) or other "collectively shared expectations" (Katzenstein 1996, 7). These two idea types play a particularly strong role in guiding actors to develop policy solutions in response to institutionally created problems such as agricultural surpluses. For instance, normative frameworks work to constrain the options that policy makers even consider as they prevent policy makers from considering solutions that do not align with their previous understandings of the world. Cognitive paradigms, on the other hand, tend to lead policy makers toward particular solutions through their focus on the cause-and-effect process and can develop as new evidence arises to correct or create new understandings of these processes. As such, we can understand them as a more explicit description of Heclo's idea of puzzling, as cognitive paradigms can shape the types of solutions policy makers deem most likely to work.

This project explores the way in which ideas and interests interact to create policy, specifically how choices about supporting national agriculture interacted with a wide variety of ideas that were explicitly used by different actors to create a program type that has taken hold around the world. The emergence of this program depends on the interaction of a variety of factors, including the specific policy choices countries made to support their agricultural industries, fears for national security, concerns with women's employment, ideas about economic theory, and ideas about the state's responsibility for its citizens. However, school lunch programs would not have come into existence were it not for two developments: a conception of childhood as distinct from adulthood and necessitating protection, and the advent of family policy, which represents the intervention of the state into the family and a growing comfort with that intervention by society and the state. Thus, while the particular ideational factors differed in the European countries and U.S. agricultural interests were paramount in the development of WFP school lunch programs, understanding the development of childhood as an idea is necessary for explaining program emergence globally.

CHILDHOOD

In order for states to make interventions into children's health, childhood had to be recognized as distinct from adulthood and children had to be valued in some way. State concern with children's health did not begin until the late nineteenth century. The conceptualization of childhood as a distinctive period in a person's life operates as an important part of Weber's ideal interests in the background of debates over school lunch programs, in that this particular conception of childhood can be understood as a normative value that actors both strive toward and can use to make arguments. In addition to a particular conception of childhood as separate from adulthood, the development of the protection of children also depended on valuing children in a new way. The first is the emotional value that children acquired and the second is the importance ascribed to children for the future of the state. Both of these trends developed in the late nineteenth and early twentieth centuries and were a necessary precondition for the change in the state-family relations that school meal programs represent. If children were not valued as children, then there would be no reason to create programs that supported them specifically as children. The conception of childhood as distinct and special has had a continuing impact on the development and prevalence of state-sponsored child welfare programs.

Childhood and adulthood were likely always somewhat separate spheres of time, but it was not until the last three hundred years that childhood began to be understood as a particular time in a person's life with particular requirements. John Locke and Jean-Jacques Rousseau first began to change attitudes toward children through their work. For instance, Locke presumes that "children lack what adult human beings possess" and thus must "be educated and brought to reason" (Archard 2004, 3), while Rousseau asserted the "right of a child to be a child and to be happy in it" (Cunningham 2005, 63). The Romantic poets, authors, and artists began to depict children, at the end of the eighteenth century, as innocent, happy, and vulnerable. These Romantic influences carried on into the nineteenth and early twentieth centuries, and it was this conception of childhood that lent credence to the argument that childhood ought to be protected from the vagaries of the adult world.

During the nineteenth and twentieth centuries, children were largely valued by the state as future manpower. Initial state involvement in education was "seen as a means of bringing order and discipline to a population and of training it in useful work skills" (Cunningham 2005, 119) and sought to "produce youth who would be serviceable to the state and its economy" (Zuckerman 2003, 231). Concern with children's welfare was largely that of concern for future citizens "who must be trained for their eventual roles in society" (Archard 2004, 155). Children have been "caught up in the international rivalry of states" because they are seen as "the most valuable asset a nation has," which must be properly nurtured and maintained so that the state itself will not degenerate compared to other countries (Cunningham 2005, 179). It was inevitable that states would begin to take a larger part in child policy.

While children began to be valued by the state for their future worth, children began to be valued differently by their families, at least for the middle classes and upper classes in Western countries. Viviana Zelizer documents the emergence of an economically worthless but emotionally priceless child in *Pricing the Priceless Child: The Changing Social Value of Children* (1985). She presents compelling evidence that, by the mid-nineteenth century, at least for the American urban middle classes, children were no longer seen as objects of utility whose worth could be measured by how much work and money the child could give the family, but as objects of sentiment upon which families, in fact, spent extra money. While the lower classes lagged behind this development, child labor laws and compulsory education pulled even lower-class children out of the economy by the 1930s, at the latest. Authors give a variety of explanations for this change, including the "success of industrial capitalism at the turn of the century which required a skilled, educated labor force" (Zelizer 1985, 8). While others focused on changes in the family, at heart this is also an economic argument as "increasing differentiation between economic production and the home transformed the basis of family cohesion. As instrumental ties weakened, the emotional value of all family members—including children—gained new saliency" (Zelizer 1985, 8–9). Others argue that lowered rates of infant mortality had a larger effect on the emotional value of children; as children were more likely to live, parents were more likely to invest emotionally in them. No matter the reason, children of all classes by the 1930s had become more emotionally valued than economically valued, which was a great change from earlier periods. This change corresponded with the conception of childhood detailed above and was complemented by the value children were seen to have for the state.

The changes in conceptions of childhood and of the value of children, both emotionally and for the state, explain the emergence of state systems

of protection for children. These protections include compulsory education, juvenile courts, child labor laws, infant welfare, and institutions to
deal with child poverty. However, it was the combination of the new conception of childhood and the new value of children that changed the purpose of child policy to that of saving children for childhood. While these
systems of child protection were initially run by philanthropic organizations, states grew increasingly involved. Cunningham argues that this was
due to a decline of confidence in the family; "it was certainly no longer
assumed that the rearing of children could simply be left to families with
the state or voluntary organizations picking up casualties" (Cunningham
2005, 155).

Much of the research on childhood has depended on Western models and Western empirical evidence. However, these models of childhood
and subsequent increase in state involvement in child welfare did have an
effect on other parts of the world. The development of the idea of children's
rights gained salience in an international body of opinion and in the development of various international organizations devoted to children's rights.
This includes, for instance, the abolition of child labor in the charter of the
International Labor Organization and the creation of the Save the Children
Fund in 1919, the declaration on Children's Rights adopted by the League
of Nations in 1924, followed by the U.N. Declaration on the Rights of the
Child in 1959 and the Convention on the Rights of the Child of 1989. Likewise, compulsory education, while certainly starting in the West, has spread
to most developing countries (Boli, Ramirez, and Meyer 1985). Thus, Western conceptions and values of childhood and children had an important
part to play in legitimating governmental involvement in children's health
and food. Today, the protection of this ideal has been formalized at the
international level, and the protection of childhood both serves as a ral-
lying cry for activists and a tool to be manipulated by political actors. The
conceptualization of childhood as a distinctive phase from adulthood that
deserves special attention by the state can be considered an important ideal
interest that worked to shape policy makers' response to issues such as child
hunger. The development of this idea was a necessary factor, or precondition, in the creation of school lunch programs, as it is highly unlikely that
programs that focused solely on feeding children would have received state
support without this shift in ideal interests in the Western world in the late
nineteenth century.

PLAN OF THE BOOK

This book uses historical comparative case study methods to analyze each phase of school lunch program emergence around the world, drawing on archival data from the United States and the U.N.'s World Food Programme, interviews with officials in Norway, India, and at the WFP, and historical agricultural statistics from the U.N.'s Food and Agricultural Organization. The second chapter considers the policy literature on school lunches and the potential of these programs to improve problems such as education, hunger, and development. This chapter rejects a rationalist explanation for school lunch program emergence based on the creation of compulsory education and explores the different types of agricultural policy, as differences in the choices of policy-makers as to how to support their agricultural sector are key to the creation of school lunch programs.

The third chapter turns to regional analysis and engages in comparative historical research to explore the question of why certain European states created school lunch programs while others did not. Conventional theories of the welfare state would suggest that only social democratic states would have created feeding programs while states that fit the liberal, conservative, or Mediterranean typologies would not. Moreover, theories suggest that levels of democracy, poverty, or party politics could play a decisive role in the creation of social policy. However, based on careful process tracing through four case studies, this chapter shows that a variety of factors were necessary in certain European countries in order to explain the creation of school lunch programs.

The fourth chapter examines the creation of the U.S. National School Lunch Program, where the factors of security and agricultural surpluses interacted. This policy innovation depended on the ability of policy entrepreneurs to link the economic concerns of agricultural production with the ideational concern of national security, which was culturally resonant as the country emerged from World War II. Agricultural surpluses had been created as the government responded to farmers' demands during the Great Depression and were able to be harnessed by southern Democrats, child welfare reformers, nutritionists, and the military to represent their interests. The policy window of World War II and the worry with national security meant that these different actors were able to frame school lunch as a security measure and assure the creation of the program. This chapter also compares the United States with its northern neighbor, Canada, as Canada did not create a school meal program despite having many of the same material conditions as the United States. This comparison helps highlight the importance of differing ideational factors in the creation and non-creation of this policy.

The fifth chapter uses archival data from the U.S. government and transcripts from the U.N. conferences that created the U.N.'s World Food Programme to focus on the relationship between the United States and WFP. In particular, this chapter shows that patterns of support for U.S. agricultural production—in combination with a new cognitive paradigm that saw children as "human capital," that is, useful for a country's development—created an incentive for the WFP to promote school feeding programs.

The sixth chapter explores the ways in which current state efforts to feed children, led by the WFP and World Bank, now prioritize market solutions to the problem of child hunger. In particular, the WFP and several African countries, including Nigeria, Kenya, and Ghana, are bolstering local agricultural production through local purchases for school lunch programs (Home-Grown School Feeding), while in much of Latin America school feeding has been replaced by the rise of conditional cash transfer programs, which give cash directly to families in exchange for school attendance. Using data from the WFP and the World Bank, this chapter demonstrates that these changes in food provision can be traced back to the development of the cognitive paradigm of post-neoliberal economics, used in conjunction with the paradigm of human capital theory.

The conclusion considers the theoretical and policy implications of this argument and focuses on the ways in which policy reflects and creates public values, as well as the limitations of current theoretical frameworks for understanding the broad array of social policy. Further, this chapter suggests that the study of school lunches demonstrates the emergence of a new norm of public responsibility to feed children and considers the effects of the new methods of school feeding, either Home-Grown School Feeding or conditional cash transfers, on women's ability to achieve social citizenship.

CONCLUSION

Over the last hundred years, states around the world have begun to provide children with lunches at school subsidized by the state or international organizations. While social policy scholars have studied early childhood development programs, they have largely ignored school lunch programs. This is an unfortunate oversight as school lunch programs represent an overlap between agricultural, educational, social, and foreign policy. School lunch programs provide a point of analysis to understand how the different interests and goals of these policy arenas interact. In other words, in order to understand the emergence of school lunches, we must examine the interaction of different policy arenas. In this case, the choices countries made regarding agricultural, educational, employment, family, and social policy all played a role in the creation or non-creation of school lunch programs. In addition, school lunch programs are a point of overlap between the family and the state—a point at which families expect the state not only to educate their child but also to help them feed their child. The physical and symbolic importance of food makes this an extremely useful subject with which to analyze the political relationship between families and the state.

Through a global survey of school lunch programs and case studies, this book demonstrates that a combination of material and ideational factors interacted in both country-specific and global contexts to produce school lunches as global social policy. In many ways, school lunch program emergence was largely an unintended by-product of particular choices policy makers made about how to protect and promote their agricultural industries. The creation of school lunch programs was dependent on an interaction between this material factor of agricultural surpluses and a variety of ideational factors that actors were able to harness in order to argue for these programs. The following chapters explore this interaction by analyzing the historical creation of school lunch programs and reflect on their utility of for addressing child hunger.

2 · HUNGER, EDUCATION, AND AGRICULTURE

Over the last hundred and fifty years, hunger became recognized as a social problem against which governments should act. Prior to the conceptualization of hunger as a humanitarian problem and then a social problem, hunger was considered a given or a punishment for those too immoral or lazy to acquire food (Vernon 2007). The reframing of hunger as a social problem reflected the efforts of reformers who first constructed the hungry as "objects of humanitarian sympathy . . . in the middle of the nineteenth century" (Vernon 2007, 38) and as such slowly created the idea that the state should be responsible for addressing hunger. This new conviction was reflected in the efforts of the early welfare states, as governments created industrial canteens, collective feeding centers, and school lunch programs. Most of these other feeding programs have been replaced by food stamp systems, but school feeding has remained as an important and integral part of hunger-alleviation efforts.

While the amount and kinds of food served in a school meal varies by country, the basic goal of all these programs is to provide food in schools with the hope that these meals will increase attendance and attention spans, improve students' cognitive foundations, and reduce hunger. This chapter explores the importance of school lunches as a policy solution to a variety of issues, including education, hunger, and development, and rejects an explanation for the emergence of school lunch programs as being related to compulsory education laws. In addition, this chapter presents an overview of the various ways in which agriculture can be subsidized. While not an explicit goal of most school lunch programs today, agricultural policies played an important role in the historical creation of school lunches. The politics that drove agricultural policy choices in different country contexts helps explain the variation in school lunch program emergence, particularly in the early stages of program creation.

HUNGER

Despite the efforts of national governments and the international community, hunger remains a pressing concern in the world today. According to the Food and Agriculture Organization (FAO)'s 2014 *State of Food Insecurity in the World Report*, 805 million people in the world are hungry, and more than 100 million children are malnourished. Despite these dire numbers, there has been some improvement in levels of malnutrition since the beginning of the Millennium Development Goals campaign: between 1990 and 2010 the percentage of malnourished children in the world dropped from 25 percent to 16 percent. Eastern Asia experienced some of the greatest declines in child malnutrition, while southern Asia and sub-Saharan Africa both experienced less drastic declines.

Most broadly defined, hunger describes "feelings of discomfort that is the body's signal that it is in need of more food" (Weisfeld-Adams and Andrzejewski 2008). As it is a feeling, hunger is an inherently subjective experience, and hunger can have different meanings and solutions in different temporal and spatial contexts (Weinreb 2012). In an attempt to avoid the contextual nature of hunger and highlight the clinical nature of the condition, the WFP and the FAO have defined hunger as a condition "in which people lack the required nutrients (protein, energy, and vitamins and minerals)" for fully productive lives, and malnutrition as the clinical condition that occurs "when people experience either nutritional deficiencies (undernutrition) or an excess of certain nutrients (overnutrition)" (WFP 2006). Likewise, undernourishment is "the condition of people whose dietary energy consumption is continuously below a minimum requirement" for fully productive lives (WFP 2006). While acknowledging the contingent nature of hunger, this book explores hunger through the more clinical lens of the WFP.

The WFP's view that hunger hinders a productive life can be illustrated by considering hunger through the lens of human needs and rights. In 1985, in an attempt to understand human welfare beyond the traditional economic model of welfare with its emphasis on resources (income, wealth, command over commodities) or utility (happiness, satisfaction, desire fulfillment), Amartya Sen proposed the linked concepts of human functioning and capabilities. Building on this, Martha Nussbaum argued that it is the capability to function, not actual functioning that "should be the goal of legislation and public planning" (1992, 221) and presents a list of ten central human functional capabilities. These capabilities are life, bodily health, bodily integrity, senses, imagination and thought, emotions, practical reason, affiliation, other species, play, and control over one's environment (Nussbaum 1992; 2000). This list "isolates those human capabilities that can be convincingly argued to be of central importance in any human life, whatever else the person chooses to pursue" (Nussbuam 2000, 74).

Len Doyal and Ian Gough have challenged Nussbaum's interpretation of capabilities by distinguishing between needs and wants. *Needs* refer to those goals that are universalizable due to the objective harm that is likely to result should that need not be satisfied, while *wants* "derive from an individual's particular preferences and cultural environment" (Gough, Wood, et al. 2004, 17). Thus, needs are those universal prerequisites that enable participation in life, which Doyal and Gough identify as physical health and autonomy. Their list of items that will, cross-culturally and universally, meet these needs include "adequate nutritional food and water, adequate protective housing, appropriate healthcare, security in childhood, significant primary relationships, physical and economic security, safe birth control and child bearing, and appropriate basic and cross-cultural education" (Gough, Wood, et al. 2004, 18). Since nutrition can be considered to be a part of Nussbaum's category of life and bodily health, we see complementarities between the two lists such that nutrition can be considered a basic human need.

Not only is food a basic human need, but it is a human right. Human rights are "literally the rights that one has simply because one is a human being" (Donnelly 2003, 10). Nutrition is a human right because it would be impossible to live a life at all, and particularly a life of dignity, without nourishment. The human right to food is recognized in the Universal Declaration of Human Rights in Article 25: "Everyone has the right to a standard of living adequate for the health and well-being of himself and his family, including food, clothing, housing, and medical care and necessary social services." The right to food is also recognized in Article 11 of the International Covenant on Economic, Social, and Cultural Rights in similar language to the Universal Declaration:

1. The State Parties to the present Covenant recognize the right of everyone to adequate food, clothing and housing and the continuous improvement of living conditions. The State Parties will take appropriate steps to ensure the realization of this right, recognizing to this effect the essential importance of international cooperation based on free consent.

2. The State Parties to the present Covenant, recognizing the fundamental right of everyone to be free from hunger, shall take, individually and through international cooperation, the measure, including specific programs, which are needed:

   a. To improve the methods of production, conservation, and distribution of food by making full use of technical and scientific knowledge, by disseminating knowledge of the principles of nutrition and by developing or reforming agrarian systems in such a way as to achieve the most efficient development and utilization of natural resources

   b. Taking into account the problems of both food-importing and food-exporting countries, to ensure an equitable distribution of world food supplies in relation to need.

The right to food is further bolstered by the Universal Declaration on the Eradication of Hunger and Malnutrition, which was adopted by the World Food Conference in 1974. The declaration focuses on problems with food production in the developing world and solutions to that, but the first principle stated is that the current food crisis (arguably continuing today) "acutely jeopardizes the most fundamental principles and values associated with the right to life and human dignity as enshrined in the Universal Declaration of Human Rights." Further, the conference proclaims, "Every man, woman and child has the inalienable right to be free from hunger and malnutrition in order to develop fully and maintain their physical and mental faculties."

At the World Food Summit in 1996, the heads of state "reaffirmed the right of everyone to have access to safe and nutritious food, consistent with the right to adequate food and fundamental right of everyone to be free from hunger."[1] This was followed by the Voluntary Guidelines to Support the Progressive Realization of the Right to Adequate Food in the Context of National Food Security in 2004, which was created by an Intergovernmental Working Group founded during the World Food Summit: Five Years Later. In addition, in September 2000, the U.N. Commission on Human Rights created a Special Rapporteur on the Right to Food, with the mandate to "examine, monitor, and report on the implementation of the right to food to the Commission, as well as to promote the conceptual development of the right to food" (Eide and Kracht 2005, 210).

There are twenty-two countries that have either explicitly declared a Right to Food in their national constitutions or whose national constitutions have been interpreted over the years to include a right to food.[2] For instance, South Africa explicitly makes provision for the right to food by requiring the state to take reasonable legislative action to realize everyone's right to food with a particular focus on state responsibility for children's and prisoners' nutrition (Eide and Kracht 2005, 111), and in Brazil, a constitutional reform was passed in 2003 inserting an explicit right to food as part of the social rights of every citizen. In states such as Uganda and India, the right to food is less explicit but has been read into the constitution over the years.

We also find a right to food listed specifically for children. One of the strongest statements on the right to food is found the Convention on the Rights of the Child. Both the Geneva Declaration of the Rights of the Child (1924) and the 1959 Declaration of the Rights of the Child contain explicit provisions mandating the feeding of children. The Geneva Declaration states that "the child that is hungry must be fed"[3] and the Declaration of the Rights of the Child contains principle 4:

4. The child shall enjoy the benefits of social security. He shall be entitled to grow and develop in health; to this end, special care and protection shall be provided to both him and to his mother, including adequate pre-natal and post-natal care. The child shall have the right to adequate nutrition, housing, recreation, and medical service.[4]

While neither of these instruments was hard law of any sort, they arguably laid the groundwork for including food in the Convention on the Rights of the Child in 1990. Two articles of this convention deal with food. Article 24 states,

1. State Parties recognize the right of the child to the enjoyment of the highest attainable standard of health and to facilities for the treatment of illness and rehabilitation of health. State Parties shall strive to ensure that no child is deprived of his or her right of access to such health care services.
2. State Parties shall pursue full implementation of this right and, in particular, shall take appropriate measures:

   a. To combat disease and malnutrition, including within the framework of primary health care, through, inter alia, the application of readily available technology and through the provision of adequate nutritious food sand clean drinking-water.

And, in article 27,

1. State Parties recognize the right of every child to a standard of living adequate for the child's physical, mental, spiritual, moral and social development.
2. The parents or others responsible for the child have the primary responsibility to secure, within their abilities and financial capacities, the conditions of living necessary for the child's development.
3. State Parties, in accordance with national conditions and their means, shall take appropriate measures to assist parents and others responsible for the child to implement this right and shall in case of need provide material assistance and support programs, particularly with regard to nutrition, clothing and housing.[5]

Thus, we see that food can be considered both a need and a right, and as such subject to legislation and policy making (Nussbaum 1992). However, these various international human rights documents give little signal as to *how* to fulfill the right to food, merely indicating that governments should be responsible when families fail.

While laying responsibility on governments for the alleviation of hunger is relatively novel, it is also deserved as so often politics and policy are responsible for hunger in the first place. While natural disaster can affect the likelihood of hunger in a household, other determinants are more directly decided by politics and include, at the national level war, levels of food production, functioning food markets, sanitation, health facilities,

and access to water. The disempowerment of women has an important effect on hunger, as parents' level of education, and particularly the
mother's education level, is important for predicting child malnutrition.
In addition, household access to food markets is particularly important.
While the most direct cause of malnutrition is inadequate dietary intake
and/or disease, you cannot divorce that immediate cause from the underlying and basic causes, which forces us to pay attention to a general lack
of resources, inadequate care for women and children, and insufficient
health services.

Hunger has a number of social and economic costs. Undernutrition is
a leading cause of child deaths worldwide due to the number of infectious
diseases that are associated with malnutrition and accounts for "7 of the 13
leading risk factors associated with the global burden of disease" (U.N. Millennium Project Task Force on Hunger 2005, 29). Undernutrition causes
poor cognitive development, especially if the malnutrition occurs in the
first two years of life, and has been shown to result in "lower productive and
lifetime earnings potential"; it is estimated that "the foregone GDP is some-
where between six and ten percent" (U.N. Millennium Project Task Force
on Hunger 2005, 29–30). This alone is a compelling reason for the creation
of feeding programs.

Undernutrition among children is particularly prevalent and problematic. In developing countries, 26 percent of children are underweight
for their age, although there are regional differences. As indicated above,
childhood malnourishment leads to cognitive losses, followed by productivity losses. Most previous research, both social science and technical,
has focused on the provision of food to children under the age of two, and
has focused on the promotion of breastfeeding. A great deal of research
indicates that zero to two are the most important years for creating mental capacity. Low birthweight, growth faltering, micronutrient deficiency,
and inadequate stimulation are all problems that lead to reduced mental
capacity and that are extremely important to address before the age of two.
Hunger during pregnancy and in the first two years of life strongly influences future mental capacity. Interventions during early childhood are particularly important for lifelong learning and can include food supplements,
micronutrient fortification, ante- and postnatal care, exclusive breastfeeding for the first six months, and education about stimulation.

SCHOOL LUNCH PROGRAMS AS A SOLUTION

While hunger has its greatest impact on mental capacity during these younger years, opportunities to learn are greatly affected by hunger at school age (World Food Program 2006, 39). Not only does hunger lead to reduced attention spans, but parents are often reluctant to send children to school because of the loss of income that will result from that child not working for the family during the school day. Interventions for school-aged children need to change the parents' views about the value of schooling. In other words, interventions need to "offset the opportunity costs of sending children to school" and can include "school feeding, take-home rations, cash transfers, and reduced fees (combined with investments in educational infrastructure and capacity)" (WFP 2006, 17). School lunch programs in particular can work to overcome some of this reluctance. One of the strongest findings of lunch program evaluations has been that school lunch programs are particularly good at increasing attendance, particularly for girls (Village Hope 2008, 2).

School attendance can be useful in fighting poverty as it has been shown to strengthen the cognitive foundation that will be used to improve availability, access, and use of nutrients. Schooling offers specific skills and knowledge about health, nutrition, sanitation, and farming, all of which can be used later in life to address future hunger (WFP 2006, 52). Empirical data shows that as level of schooling rises, gross domestic product likewise increases (WFP 2006, 52). Thus, school lunch programs are thought of as an integral part of improving human capital as they function to entice children to school, with the assumption that, once educated, they will improve both their lot in life as well as contribute to their country's economic development. This is the core tenet of human capital theory, which became important to the development of school feeding programs by the WFP.

However, school lunch programs on their own cannot improve human capital if other factors such as school infrastructure, teacher quality, and laws supporting primary education are not in place. In fact, school lunches can sometimes have a negative effect on education because increased attendance leads to school crowding. In addition, the influx of new students to schools can sometimes slow the learning process as these students, having suffered malnutrition, are more likely to be slower learners (WFP 2006). However, even with these caveats, the available evidence strongly suggests that school lunch programs consistently reduce short-term hunger and improve school attendance (Greenlagh, Kristjansson, and Robinson 2007; Miller del Rosso 1999; Village Hope 2008).

School feeding runs the gamut from breakfast porridge to a mid-morning snack to a meal at midday to take-home rations such as a bag of rice and a can of oil. It varies by country, with developed countries being more likely to provide a full sit-down meal focused around hot food and developing countries more likely to rely on snacks or take-home rations. National food culture is often reflected in the meals: for instance, the meals in Italy are centered around pastas or risottos with meat only appearing on the plates a few times a week, while for lunch in Korea kim chi and rice are almost always offered. In the United States, the lunches almost always include a meat entrée,[6] while in India the meals, needing to appeal to Hindus and Muslims alike, are primarily vegetarian. In some countries where the WFP works, only nutritional biscuits are offered. The meals reflect not only the food culture but the economic reality of each country. All of them are designed to encourage children to eat at school in order to improve their capacity to learn. While this is a goal of most school feeding programs, particularly those in developing countries, it was not necessarily the primary intention of early school feeding programs, and uncovering the dynamics other than hunger that led to the creation of these programs provides the basis for the rest of this book.

EDUCATION AS AN ALTERNATIVE EXPLANATION

The strong results connecting school meals and increased attendance suggest a potential explanation for the creation of school lunch programs, which is a rationalist argument that sees parents demanding lunches if their children are being forced to go to school. This argument is explicated in British news articles published around the time of Britain's compulsory education law; letters to the editor of *The Times* of London in the early 1900s express support for school meals based on the argument that "if children are compelled by the State to attend school, the State should also be compelled to feed them" (*The Times* 1905). This argument sees parents and/

or society demanding responsibility from the state for the physical health of children when the state begins to take responsibility for the intellectual health of children, and would suggest that school lunch programs emerged at the same time as compulsory education.

However, this argument is not supported by the data. After compiling the dates at which a country adopted a compulsory education law and comparing those to the dates of school lunch program adoption, there is very little evidence to support this hypothesis. There are just seven countries that created school lunch programs within five years of the compulsory education law. These countries are Grenada, Hungary, Ireland, Israel, Japan, Nigeria, and Venezuela. Of these, Hungary, Israel, and Japan created the school lunch program either at the time of compulsory education law's passage or within a year. In those three cases, I do think there is a plausible causal connection between the law and the school lunch program. Namibia created a lunch program within ten years of the compulsory education law, while another four countries, Bangladesh, Chile, Egypt, and Mongolia, created a school lunch program within twenty years of the compulsory education law. After twenty years, it seems unlikely that parents would be so upset about an issue that they would insist on the creation of a school lunch program.

Further evidence that compulsory education laws do not explain the creation of school lunch programs comes from the nine countries that started school lunch programs *before* a compulsory education law existed. These countries are Barbados, Bolivia, Colombia, Cuba, Kuwait, Malaysia, Romania, South Africa, and Sri Lanka. In addition, three countries have school lunch programs and still do not have a compulsory education law (Botswana, Brunei Darussalam, and Jamaica) while another eighteen countries have World Food Programme school lunch programs but no compulsory education laws.[7] Finally, all but two of the countries that do *not* have school lunch programs have compulsory education laws.

A rationalist explanation that sees school lunch programs as simply a corollary of education is mistaken. While both compulsory education and school lunches represent an intrusion or an extension of state power into the family, intellectual health and physical health are obviously regarded as separate areas. While educational policy, and particularly the decisions made by states about the length of the school day, played an important role in some European states' decisions to create school lunch programs, compulsory education cannot on its own explain them.

A ROLE FOR AGRICULTURE

While there is no causal link between education and school lunch program emergence, there is a plausible link between school lunch program emergence and national agricultural policy. School lunches are obviously dependent on agricultural goods in order to exist. However, it is not enough to simply correlate agricultural production with school lunch program emergence. This reveals an obvious mismatch as a large number of agricultural-importing states chose to create school lunch programs. Instead, we must examine agricultural policies in a nuanced manner and explore the variety of ways that states use to protect and promote their agricultural industries. The variety of methods employed by states to support agriculture vary by time and place, and are largely determined by different political considerations, pressures, and blocs in each country. This variation necessitates an understanding of the policy tools used to support agriculture as well as an analysis of the politics behind agricultural policy.

Generally, agricultural policy has the following objectives: "increasing farm incomes, stabilizing agricultural markets, providing an adequate supply of food, improving agricultural productivity, and, in the case of developing countries, providing cheap food and fiscal revenues for general economic development" (Miner and Hathaway 1988, 46). While most countries have similar agricultural policy objectives, there are vast differences in whether countries prioritized production or farmers' incomes, which would have great effect on the creation of school lunches as countries that prioritized production were much more likely to create a school meal program due to the need to consume excess agricultural products.

Further, there are large differences between how developed and developing countries manage their agricultural policy. Developed countries typically provide large subsidies to their agricultural industries, while developing countries tend to heavily tax their agricultural industries. This is a historical pattern that can be traced back to at least the 1860s (Lindert 1991, 72). Following World War II, developed countries embraced international markets and adopted domestic policies that were favorable to international markets, while developing countries "adopted trade policies that greatly reduced the ties between their domestic markets and the international economy" (Valdes 1991, 94). This difference, which resulted in more large-scale food production in developed countries, partly explains why the possibilities for school lunches appeared first in developed countries, where the necessary material, food, was more likely to be available rather than in developing countries, which did not prioritize or support agricultural production.

There are a number of theories to explain the high level of agricultural subsides in developed countries, including a desire for food security and nostalgia for the farm, but it is generally agreed that the best explanation is that the shrinking number of farmers and the consolidation of farmers into corporate holdings in developed countries leads to a stronger political pull via the creation of agricultural interest groups. Mancur Olson explains this phenomenon through the logic of collective action and the effectiveness of small groups (Olson 1965 [2003], 53): in other words, "small sectors lobby powerfully" (Lindert 1991, 74). Even though the power of agricultural interest groups in the developed world varies by place and time, these organized groups have often had a large impact on the creation of policy that is favorable to farmers (Sheingate 2003). For example, in the United States farmers successfully pressed for special protection time and again, resulting in an extensive system of subsidies even as the number of farmers diminished (Winders 2009). This theory not only explains why developed countries are more likely to subsidize agriculture, but it also partly explains why developing countries are more likely to tax agriculture: in developing countries with a large number of scattered farmers, these farmers are less likely to be able to work together to lobby their government for favorable policies.

High taxation of agriculture in developing countries began early, as states taxed their agricultural sectors in order to finance rapid industrial development (Gerschenkron 1962). It was believed that growth in agriculture was unnecessary and that industrial growth was the best way to achieve economic development. Along with a pro-urban bias (Lipton 1977), there continues to be strong protection of industry in developing countries with the consequent result of "distorted incentives against the production of tradable agricultural goods" (Valdes 1991, 97). In addition, if we assume that governments are interested in creating revenue, either for the self-interest of politicians or for the support of state services, then we can assume that governments with greater pressure to raise revenue (developing countries) will tax exports and imports highly. Thus, the anti-trade bias of a developing country's agricultural policy is best explained by the demand of the state for revenue (Lindert 1991, 74) and the lack of power possessed by a large number of small farmers. This problem is further exacerbated when developing countries focus on the production of other natural resources that are likely to generate quicker revenue, such as oil or valuable minerals. This further devalues agriculture while leaving these countries vulnerable to the boom-bust cycle of Dutch disease (Kahl 2006). Further, the protectionist policies of developed countries lower global prices for agricultural goods, making it difficult for agricultural producers in developing countries to stay competitive (Stiglitz 2002). While recent decisions on agricultural policy from the World Trade Organization are meant to address some of these trade imbalances, evidence indicates that developed countries are continuing their protectionist policies even while developing countries are attempting to reduce their trade policy distortions (Anderson 2006).

In developed countries, there has historically been a much stronger farm bloc demanding support and concessions. However, the kinds of support that were provided varied, largely due to country-specific political factors, which would reverberate in the kinds of policy decisions made about feeding children. Historically, developed states have used a broad range of protectionist measures such as price supports, deficiency payments, subsidizing agricultural inputs, subsidizing food prices, import quotas, and tariff barriers. Even today, despite the calls for free trade under the World Trade Organization, most states maintain high levels of protection for agriculture.

The current global agricultural regime was put in place following World War II as countries attempted to bounce back from the disruption the war caused to agricultural markets. The choice of which measures would be used to protect agriculture were driven by the political calculus in each country, and often influenced by the type of policy that had been pursued during the war to maintain agricultural stocks for the troops. Following World War II, most countries pushed for increasing production and becoming self-sufficient in agriculture for both political and economic reasons, as it allowed states to save on scarce hard currency and avoid the repetition of wartime shortages in case of war with the Soviet Union (Federico 2012, 26). However, each country prioritized differently, with some choosing to focus on subsidizing agriculture in an effort to build up their agricultural exports, some focusing on stabilizing farmers' income, and some focusing on becoming self-sufficient.

While there are many ways that governments can support their agricultural industries, the two major ones include price support policies and direct payments. Under price support policies, the government creates an artificially high guaranteed minimum price for a commodity that protects the farmer from the fluctuations of the commodity markets. Governments set that price and then, if needed, buy up excess commodities to resell on the market themselves. While these policies are often accompanied by production controls, or restrictions on production in an effort to avoid surpluses, farmers respond to the incentives and often find ways around these production restrictions (Winders 2009). As such, these types of programs often result in government surpluses. The second method was to support the farmers themselves by offering essentially a farmers' wage that would usually be commensurate with industrial wages. This was usually accomplished through what is called a deficiency payment, whereby farmers are simply paid the difference between the government-supported price and the market price. These policies were designed to keep people on the farm in order to produce products for the country and rarely resulted in surpluses, as there was not the same kind of market distortion that occurred under price support policy.

The differences in the ways in which countries choose to support agriculture leads to a more nuanced hypothesis. It seems likely that school lunch programs would emerge in countries where agricultural policy encouraged domestic production rather than supporting farmers. Certainly there was a precedent for this link between agricultural and school feeding; in several countries, school lunch programs were preceded by school milk programs, which were deliberately created to appease agricultural interests. For instance, in 1924 the United Kingdom began providing free milk in all schools to all children. This move followed encouragement from the government to increase milk production in order to stave off threats from imports. As a result, milk was heavily subsidized and overproduced (Wibberley 2008); schools provided an ideal location to dispose of this overproduction. Likewise, milk was made available in public schools in Norway as early as 1935, and its appearance can be traced back to the subsidies that began in 1935. The dairy industry was one of the few agricultural industries singled out for a price support subsidy system in 1935 as a result of a political deal between the Labour and Agrarian parties to increase milk prices (Andresen and Elvbakken 2007, 376). The dairy industry had been particularly affected by falling prices and surplus production during the interwar years, and milk became an important political symbol of the alliance between the urban and rural areas (Kjærnes 2003).

These two examples suggest that we must consider not only the differences between the policies themselves but the politics behind the policies in order to understand the role that agriculture played in school lunch program emergence. A central contention of this book is that the material factor of agriculture, that is, the availability of the kinds of foodstuffs that could be used in school meals, was a necessary though not sufficient factor in the creation of school lunch programs, at both the national and international level. Therefore, in unveiling the politics behind the choices different countries have made in supporting their agricultural sector, we can begin to understand the puzzle of school lunches.

CONCLUSION

The choices that different countries made to support their agricultural industries is an important factor in the creation of school lunch programs, particularly in the creation of these programs in Europe, the United States, and subsequently the World Food Programme. These choices created the material factor that allowed for the possibility of lunches, as there was enough food to use for this purpose. However, other factors, particularly ideational ones, mattered as well. It was not enough to simply have policies that could or did create surpluses, but rather that governments chose to use those surpluses in support of feeding children. There are any number of ways to use excess food, including selling it on the export market, creating food-for-work programs, donating it to other countries as emergency food aid, holding onto it for the future, or dumping the products on other countries' markets. In fact, all of these uses for agricultural surpluses did and do happen. Using food to feed children was the result of particular political action by those who cared about feeding children. Ideas about national security, women, welfare, and the economy were necessary to convince governments to use food in this particular way and were used by actors in order to press for and justify the creation of lunch programs. In Western Europe, ideas related to the role of women, welfare, and national security played a particularly important role in encouraging governments to set up these types of programs in the wake of World War II, and it is to these developments that we turn next.

3 · THE FIRST WAVE IN EUROPE
Women and Welfare

The earliest national school lunch programs were created in Western Europe and the United States, and that model of meal provision was subsequently spread around the world. Uncovering the roots of program creation in Western Europe provides hints of the dynamics at play during the subsequent period when the World Food Programme worked to incorporate school lunches as a development tool. However, as demonstrated in table 3.1, not all Western European countries created these programs. Why did these states create programs while others did not? Conventional explanations might focus on welfare state typologies, party politics, or levels of child poverty to explain the broad variance in program creation. However, upon examination none of these answers can explain the difference in school lunch program creation. Comparing historical case studies and historical agricultural data, we see that the interaction of key material and ideational factors resulted in the creation of these programs in these particular countries.

This chapter explores the interconnections between the following types of policy: welfare, family and gender, education, and agriculture. Following World Wars I and II, many countries made changes to their agricultural policy that created much more protectionist regimes than had previously existed. However, these protectionist regimes varied as to whether they were primarily concerned with supporting farmer incomes or building up production. In those countries focused on building up

TABLE 3.1 The European Puzzle

Program Created/Year	No Program Created (to This Day)
United Kingdom (1906) 1944[a]	Austria
Finland 1948	Belgium
France 1932	Germany
Italy 1953	Greece
Ireland 1931	Netherlands
Portugal 1948	Norway
Spain mid-1940s	Switzerland
Sweden 1946	Denmark

[a]The United Kingdom created a limited and local program in 1906, but did not create a national program until 1944.

production, agricultural policy created the potential for surplus goods. Actors driven by ideas about women and children, national security, or state responsibility for citizen's welfare took advantage of these potential surpluses to argue for the creation of school lunch programs. While in all countries a specific type of agricultural policy was a necessary factor in the creation of school lunch programs, gender regimes, national security, welfare, and educational time policy played varied roles, depending on a specific country's context and driving ideational concerns. This chapter explores the emergence of lunch programs in two countries (Sweden and Great Britain) and the non-emergence in two others (Norway and Germany) in order to demonstrate that agriculture should be understood as a necessary but not sufficient cause and to illustrate the way in which different ideational factors were necessary for program emergence.

FAMILY POLICY

The lack of school feeding programs across Europe is a surprise when one considers that almost all European states had had charity-driven school feeding in the late 1800s (Bryant 1913; Gunderson 1970), leading one to expect that these charity and/or city-run programs would become institutionalized as state programs, following a similar pattern as other early welfare attempts such as health services (Beito 2000). Instead, only some states created state-level feeding programs while other states backed away from feeding efforts. In addition, the creation of intensive family policy in most Western European states in the early 1900s indicates a willingness on the part of states to intervene directly in the lives of their citizens, in particular to encourage child-bearing and support women at home, which makes it surprising that some states did not create school lunch programs, which are another state-centric method of intervening directly in the lives of families.

Family policy today is wide-ranging and even when narrowly defined as those "measures directly targeted at families with dependent children" can include "family allowances, means-tested family benefits, tax relief for dependent children . . . maternity and paternity leave, child-care leave . . . day care centers, after-school care" as well as laws pertaining to education, health care, abortion, divorce, and child support payments (Gauthier 1996, 3). Family policy grew slowly in the twentieth century and in many ways only became institutionalized in both political and popular understandings in the 1960s. However, the roots of these policies are easily traced back to the turn of the century when a large number of European countries began to intervene overtly in the lives of families. In particular, governments concerned by poverty focused on improving the education of mothers regarding children, providing mothers with medical assistance, providing families with emergency cash, and creating the first maternity leave schemes (Gauthier 1996, 39). A comparative glance at European countries shows that all the countries under consideration in this chapter other than Belgium, Greece, and Iceland had created some sort of health assistance for mothers and children, usually dependent on income level, prior to 1945, and that Austria, Belgium, Denmark, Finland, France, Germany, Italy, Netherlands, Spain, Switzerland, and the United Kingdom all created widows' and orphans' pensions or some other type of cash benefit for families prior to 1945. This indicates state acknowledgment of a responsibility for the welfare of mothers and children who, at the very least, were not supported by a male breadwinner.

In most of the European countries, this idea of state responsibility for mothers and children rapidly expanded to cover families who were supported by a male breadwinner with the passage of family allowances in all

Western European countries by 1958. These schemes varied as to whether coverage was universal or employment related, and as to whether they covered all children or only from the second or third child on, but all had at their core an element of public rather than private responsibility for families. Certainly family policies, particularly those created after World War II, had an economic element, which was an attempt to avoid wage inflation (Land and Parker 1978, 345), but the programs must be understood by the nature of their intervention into the family. The programs encouraged parents to have more children, worked to reduce child poverty, and actively encouraged a male breadwinner model by providing money to cover, in theory at least, the lost wages of the nonworking mother. The universal spread of these programs, which indicate the greater willingness of the state to be involved in and actively shape families, leads one to wonder why only a handful of these countries created school lunch programs, a state intervention into the lives of families that can do a great deal of good by providing certain types of necessary nutrition and by relieving the burden on families of at least one meal a day.

CONVENTIONAL WELFARE TYPOLOGIES AND OTHER PLAUSIBLE EXPLANATIONS

Answers to these questions might be found in conventional explanations of the welfare state. These explanations, first identified by Gosta Esping-Anderson (1990), categorize states by their differing levels of the decommodification of labor and the way in which the state responds to the political demands of labor movements; the categories of social democratic, liberal, conservative/corporatist, and Mediterranean have been created to describe the different patterns of welfare activity and spending in the postwar period. However, the presence or absence of school lunch programs cannot be explained satisfactorily by the classic welfare state typologies. While many countries fit uneasily into their typological destinations (Huber and Stephens 2001; Morgan 2006), scholars have used these typologies in order to understand the different trends, structures, and impacts of welfare states (Arts and Gelissen 2002; 2010; Esping-Anderson 1990). Table 3.2 shows the countries of interest grouped into their various typologies, indicates whether or not a country has a program, and clearly reveals the discrepancies throughout the welfare typologies.

School lunch programs seem an obvious extension of the social-democratic welfare state, relying on the provision of universal benefits provided by public spending. However, Sweden and Finland have school lunch programs, while Denmark and Norway do not. In more liberal welfare regimes, which are defined by their focus on means testing and a reliance on the market for the provision of services, one would not expect school lunch programs to emerge. Yet, in the United States, Ireland, and the United Kingdom, school lunch programs have been an important part of the school day since the 1940s. One would expect the conservative/corporatist countries not to have school lunch programs, as these countries rely on the principle of subsidiarity and expect families to provide for most welfare needs, but France defies these expectations by having had a school lunch program since 1932. Finally, the Mediterranean welfare states, with their focus on the family providing assistance as well as the "dualism, fragmentation, and ineffectiveness of the social protection system" (Gal 2009, 6), would seem unlikely to have school lunch programs.[1] But, as the table shows, Italy, Spain, and Portugal all have school lunch programs. The highly variable nature by which countries incorporate school lunches into their welfare state typologies suggests the need to examine other factors.

TABLE 3.2 Conventional Welfare-State Typologies

Liberal	Conservative	Social Democratic	Mediterranean
Ireland (Y)	Austria (N)	Denmark (N)	Greece (N)
Switzerland (N)	Belgium (N)	Finland (Y)	Italy (Y)
United Kingdom (Y)	France (Y)	Norway (N)	Portugal (Y)
	Germany (N)	Sweden (Y)	Spain (Y)
	Netherlands (N)		

KEY: Y = has a school lunch program; N = does not have a school lunch program.

Child Poverty and Welfare

While conventional welfare state typologies do not explain the variance in school lunch program creation, it seems plausible that varying levels of child poverty and a concomitant support for child welfare might. Certainly the offhand rationale offered in many secondary sources on school lunch programs focuses on school lunches as a poverty-alleviation effort (Hagemann, Jarausch, and Allemann-Ghionada 2011, 20), and the programs are used for this purpose today in many developing countries. However, it has been almost impossible for scholars to find cross-national historical statistics on child poverty. While a number of local surveys were completed in different countries, there was a lack of national-level poverty statistics in the early twentieth century; however, we can extrapolate from those local surveys to make generalizations about national poverty levels. For instance, in England Charles Booth in East London (1889–1903), Benjamin Seebohm Rowntree in York (1889), and P. H. Mann in Bedfordshire (1903) all surveyed and found fairly high rates of child poverty. Local surveys continued throughout this period; the Boyd Orr survey was completed between 1937 and 1939 and covered 1,343 households in sixteen towns. The survey revealed 71.6 percent of children living in poverty (Hatton and Martin 2010). Other surveys at the time, for instance, a second survey in York by Rowntree, found 43 percent of children living in poverty (Rowntree 1941). Although the exact percentages vary, child poverty at the turn of the twentieth century was quite high cross-nationally.

While early city-based school lunch programs were driven by concerns with child poverty, this factor alone cannot explain school lunch program creation at the national level. In the first place, all these countries had high levels of child poverty, but not all countries created school lunch programs. In the second place, policy creation depends on the framing of a particular problem and solution (Stone 1989). There are many problems, but only a few of them receive attention: in order for policy action to occur, an issue must be first defined as a problem about which something can be done, rather than as a condition about which nothing can be done. This is most likely to happen when an issue violates important values, show us to be inferior to other countries or relevant political units, or are defined into a category that forces action (Kingdon 2003). Child poverty has historically attracted concern from churches and charities but very little interest from the state until it was framed such that solutions to child poverty were necessary for state goals, such as continued population growth or security (Cunningham 2005). While the existence of child poverty is likely to be a background factor for the creation of these programs, the programs were spurred by those concerned with very different factors such as national security or women's roles.

Similarly, a concern with child welfare cannot explain the variation in program creation, as the majority of states across Western Europe had regulated child labor in some way by the 1880s, passed compulsory education laws by the 1920s, and declared support for the 1924 League of Nations Declaration of Children's Rights. While many of these laws were not effective, their existence indicates some state support for, and adherence to, an idea of childhood and the protection of children's welfare. Likewise, the signing of the declaration indicates at least a normative adherence to the children's regime represented by that document. Indeed, the founder of Save the Children and the main promoter of the declaration, Englantyne Jebb, hoped the declaration would serve that normative purpose and encourage states to pay more attention to child welfare and pass laws in line with the goals it outlined (Marshall 1999, 131). Since the children's welfare regime and states' nominal adherence to it at the time which school lunch programs were being actively debated was largely uniform across Western European countries, they cannot be used to explain the variance in school lunch program emergence.

Party Politics

Another explanation might be found in party politics. It seems likely that left-leaning parties would be more supportive of the expanding social welfare programs, as these programs are in line with many of the stated political goals of the left. However, examining the historical party data from those countries that did create school lunch programs reveals a broad range of parties in power across the ideological spectrum, including conservative governments, which are not usually associated with the expansion of state services. In addition, the broad variance on this factor across both countries that created programs and those that did not suggests that party politics cannot explain program creation. Table 3.3 clearly indicates the discrepancy between party politics and program creation.

TABLE 3.3 Party Orientation

Program Created	No Program Created
Finland—left	Austria—conservative
France—conservative	Belgium—conservative
Italy—conservative	Denmark—conservative
Ireland—conservative	Germany—conservative
Portugal—conservative	Greece—conservative
Spain—conservative	Netherlands—conservative
Sweden—left	Norway—left
United Kingdom—left	Switzerland—liberal

NOTE: This table lists the party in power at the time of program creation, or in the case of those countries that did not create programs, the political orientation of the first two governments following World War II.

Educational Time Policies

A further explanation might simply be functional; that school lunch programs were an inevitable outgrowth of the varying time policies created by states to govern education: the fact that England and France created all-day schools earlier than other countries might explain why they also created school lunches. However, it is possible to build a lunch break into a school day with the expectation that children will go home for those lunches, which was, and is, the case in Norway. In fact, England and France might be seen as special cases as in France the government was concerned about keeping children away from the influences of the church (Morgan 2006), which meant that the state was invested in keeping children at school, while in England there was a strong belief that education was partly intended to create social community and that meals were an opportunity to practice that doctrine (Hagemann, Jarausch, and Allemann-Ghionada 2011, 20–21). In many other countries with all-day schools, value was seen in sending children home for lunch because they could benefit from the community created by a family meal. Meanwhile, both Spain and Italy had only half-day school programs until the 1960s but created school lunch programs. The variance on this factor suggests that a purely functional explanation of time policy will not suffice, although it does provide a motivating factor in at least two countries.

SCHOOL LUNCHES: MATERIAL AND
IDEATIONAL EXPLANATIONS

Since explanations that focus broadly on welfare type, party politics, or child poverty do not explain the creation of school lunches, we must turn to examine other factors that explain the creation of school lunches in Western Europe, including agricultural policy, gender ideology, security, and the creation of welfare states.

Agriculture

Generally speaking, the creation of school lunch programs depends on having the basic materials for school lunches, that is, food. Thus, to understand the creation of school lunch programs in Western Europe we must investigate agricultural policy in the various states at the time. This is a daunting task as there are no comparative statistics before 1960, which is when the FAO began keeping records. In order to piece together different countries' agricultural policies or outcomes I have relied largely on the secondary literature, which means that the statistics are not necessarily truly comparative, due to the variety of data collected in each country. In order to determine agricultural goals in the postwar period, I used the 1957 USDA Report *Agricultural Policies of Foreign Governments: Including Trade Policies Affecting Agriculture.* Analyzing secondary data sources from the pre- and immediate postwar period, as well as the 1957 report, gives an almost comprehensive view of the agricultural policies pursued by most Western European countries between 1935 and 1957.[2]

Following World War II, most countries pushed for increasing production and becoming self-sufficient in agriculture for both political and economic reasons. However, each country prioritized differently, with some choosing to focus on subsidizing agriculture in an effort to build up their agricultural exports, others focusing on stabilizing farmers' income, and yet others focusing on becoming self-sufficient. Generally speaking, those countries that created school lunch programs tended to privilege agricultural production over the stabilization of farm incomes, although certainly both were important goals in all cases. This is not surprising as it seems likely that school lunch programs would emerge in countries where agricultural policy created surpluses, as those surpluses could be used in lunches. Those countries that created school lunch programs had a combination of agricultural goals and pricing policy that encouraged agricultural overproduction for two key reasons: first, countries that offered price guarantees on *many* products after the war were more likely to create broad agricultural overproduction; and second, countries that had the explicit goal of producing for export or self-sufficiency after the war, instead of the goal of stabilizing farmers' incomes, were also more likely to overproduce agricultural goods.

The 1957 USDA Report makes clear the primary policy goal for each country in the immediate postwar period. These goals are listed in table 3.4. The data in this table reveal that, with the exception of Sweden, every country that created a school lunch program set specific goals to increase the production of agricultural goods. This overproduction of agricultural products was diverted into feeding programs in countries where agricultural goods were connected to other national goals that could be achieved by feeding children. Increased production alone was not sufficient to start programs as seen in Greece, Denmark, and Switzerland.

In addition, there is a strong correlation between how countries protected their markets with price supports and the creation of a school lunch program. Price support policy creates a guaranteed minimum price for a commodity

TABLE 3.4 Major Agricultural Policy Goals

Stabilize/Improve Farmers' Incomes	Increase Exports	Achieve Food Self-Sufficiency
Sweden	*France*	*Finland*
Austria	*Italy*	*Ireland*
Belgium	*Spain*	*Portugal*
Germany	Denmark	*United Kingdom*
Netherlands	Greece	Switzerland
Norway		

NOTE: Countries in italics are those that created a school lunch program. The policy goals for Ireland and France were judged on the basis of the period leading up to the initial creation of school meal programs in 1931 and 1932, respectively.

that protects the farmer from the fluctuations of the commodity markets. Governments set that price and then buy up the commodities to resell on the market themselves. These programs result in government surpluses. While agricultural surpluses can be useful, and were politically popular in many countries following World War II and the war-created fear of scarcity, the governments eventually have to dispose of surpluses. This has led to the problem of "dumping" products, particularly in developing countries, through the guise of food aid, which often has the effect of distorting local markets.

One of the other avenues for the disposal of surplus agricultural products is in local programs such as school feeding programs. The United States, as one example, has historically used its school lunch program to dispose of surplus agricultural products that it has purchased through its various price support programs (Levine 2008). All countries in the postwar period provided price guarantees on some of their products, but they differed as to whether they promised price guarantees for just a few products such as milk and butter (the most common) or for many products. There is a marked difference in the 1957 report between those countries that promised price guarantees for a few products and those that promised price guarantees for many products. The differences are shown in table 3.5.

The data in the table unequivocally demonstrate that no country that created a school lunch program had a small price guarantee policy. Countries that promised price guarantees on more products inevitably created surpluses. Interestingly, while Sweden did not list self-sufficiency or increased exports as an explicit policy goal, unlike the other countries that created programs, their use of multiple price guarantees suggests that they were trying to balance the goal of increasing production with the goal of improving farmers' incomes.

Tellingly, the data in the two tables also reveal that particular types of agricultural policy, while a necessary factor in the creation of school meal programs, cannot be considered a sufficient factor, due to the fact that several countries that did not create programs either had price supports on many goods (Germany and Belgium) or actively pursued increased agricultural exports (Denmark and Greece). These results suggest the necessity to consider additional factors.

TABLE 3.5 Price Support Policies

Price Supports on More than Three Products	Price Supports on Fewer than Three Products
Finland	Austria
France	Denmark
Italy	Greece
Spain	Ireland
Sweden	Netherlands
United Kingdom	Norway
Belgium	
Germany	
Switzerland	

NOTE: Countries in italics are those that created a school lunch program. The price support policies for Ireland and France were judged on the basis of the period leading up to the initial creation of school meal programs in 1931 and 1932, respectively.

Ideational Factors

While certain kinds of agricultural policy are a necessary factor for the creation of school lunch programs, governments had to choose to channel agricultural products into feeding programs rather than simply selling them on the open market or donating them to other countries. Agricultural policy created a basic set of possibilities or parameters for action through the creation of surpluses; actors, driven by an array of ideas, figure out how to make use of these possibilities. While the range of ideas that could influence the creation of school lunch programs in Western Europe is vast, one of the primary ideas that mattered was ideologies regarding women's roles. These can be assessed in part by comparing employment policy and, in some case cases, educational time policies. As such, gender is an essential category to consider in the creation of school lunch programs. The claim is not that school lunches radically changed gender relations after their implementation but rather that program creation (or non-creation) reflected the prevailing attitudes toward women's roles at the time.

Many countries were invested in the male breadwinner/female home-maker model, whereby any support for families was provided with the goal of maintaining this family structure (J. Lewis 1992). While scholars have spent a great deal of time classifying states into categories such as male breadwinner, separate gender roles, or individual carer-earner, with these categories evolving in sophistication over time through spirited debate (J. Lewis 1992; Sainsbury 1999), these categories are not useful for understanding school lunch programs. For instance, historically male breadwinner states such as Ireland in 1930, the United Kingdom in 1944, Italy in 1953, or Spain in the mid-1940s all created school lunch programs. What is more relevant is countries' policies toward women's employment.

States categorized as male breadwinner had very different policies toward women's employment than the title male breadwinner might suggest. For instance, France, which has long been classified as a male-breadwinner state, has a history of state support for child care and preschools owing largely to the fight between clerical and anticlerical forces in the last twenty years of the nineteenth century. Kimberly Morgan (2006) highlights the importance of ideology, and particularly religion, when considering differing rates of mothers' employment. She argues that to understand the creation of the welfare state in the 1940s in Europe, and particularly policies relating to women, we must focus on the political and religious cleavages of the previous several decades. She explores the patterns of church-state cleavages or church-state fusion to explain the prevalence of policies supporting women's employment in countries such as Sweden, Denmark, France, and Belgium, while focusing on the ways in which religious conflict, usually between several sects, has led to a lack of support for women's employment in Austria, Germany, Italy, and the Netherlands. Finally, she finds a lack of support for women's employment in the liberal countries such as the United Kingdom and United States due to religious pluralism and removal of religion from formal politics.

Therefore, in some countries official policy supported women's employment for historical religious reasons, despite their categorization as a male-breadwinner state. In France and Sweden, for example, school lunches supported the state goal of women's employment. The specifics of mothers' employment, rather than gender regimes as a whole, might better explain school lunch program creation as these programs would certainly reflect the interests of a state that was invested in supporting working mothers. Of course, countries like Italy and the United Kingdom had very low levels of public support for mothers' employment and yet created programs, while countries like Belgium and Denmark, with higher levels of support for mothers' employment, did not, which suggests that this factor was relevant in some cases but not others.

There were a number of ideas that mattered in the creation of school lunch programs in Western Europe. In addition to gender, states such as Sweden and Finland were also driven to create school lunch programs by those who saw them as an integral part of a welfare state, whereby states took on a greater responsibility for the health and welfare of their citizens. In others, the type of welfare state that reformers envisioned precluded the idea of feeding children. In states such as Germany, a concern with the promotion of individualism, as a reaction to socialism, ruled out the possibility of a school lunch program, while in Spain and Portugal, a belief in the preeminence of the state as a guiding force drove the creation of these programs. Finally, in states such as Great Britain and France, a concern with national security and the fear that child malnutrition would affect the future security of the state was a driving idea in the creation of a school lunch program. The following case studies illustrate the various pathways by which school lunch programs were created in Europe and demonstrate the importance of both material and ideational factors. In each of these case studies, agriculture is a necessary factor in program creation, while specific countries highlight different ideational factors in their own program creation. While gender is a determining factor in three of these case studies, in the fourth, Great Britain, welfare and national security are the decisive factors. Including negative case studies can be a particularly useful way to test and confirm a theory as well as to help illuminate the causal pathways of the variables in question (Mahoney and Goertz 2004; Skocpol 1979), so this section includes both positive and negative cases.

CASE STUDIES

Sweden

In many ways it is not surprising that the Swedish parliament, under social democratic control, created a school lunch program as an integral part of their welfare state in 1946. Their social democratic welfare state is composed of universal programs to aid their citizens. In addition, Sweden had, at least partially, the material factor of agricultural policies likely to produce surpluses, as well as a nascent gender ideology that prioritized equality between the genders and a strong state commitment to promote population health. While these factors make it hardly a puzzle to explain the existence of the Swedish school lunch program, it is still instructive to trace the pathways by which agricultural policy and ideas interacted to generate a school lunch program in the nascent Swedish welfare state.

While school meals had been provided since the introduction of compulsory education in the 1840s, largely through church or other philanthropic organizations for the very poor (Gullberg 2006), this broader state-funded program was explicitly designed to meet a number of goals, including social equality, gender equality, and to "foster healthy citizens" (Osowoski 2012, 10). The Social Democrats, who came into power in Sweden in 1932, put forth, in their 1928 platform, a vision of social equality that guided Sweden's welfare state for much of the twentieth century (Korsvold 2011, 140). Related to this vision of social equality was a concern with childcare and early childhood education. Alva Myrdal, a Social Democrat, helped shape the debate over the role of the state in childcare and childhood with the publication in 1934, with her husband Gunnar Myrdal, of the book *Crisis in the Population Question*. This book was written as a response to the population decline that many Western European countries were experiencing in the 1930s. The Myrdals' book advocated the creation of school meals, free health services, day care centers, and subsidized food and argued that these services would help support families and encourage those couples who were wary of the cost to have children. The Myrdals advocated services in kind, such as school meals, as the government could directly allocate resources to meet need and did not have to pay out cash from the government budget. The book was a political sensation and was read widely by politicians from all parties.

In a further effort to bolster the population rate, Sweden put in place a number of policies designed to make marriage more attractive to women. For instance, married women were allowed to dispose of their own property, were considered fully equal in marriage, and made equal property owners with husbands (Morgan 2006). In addition, the maternity relief scheme of 1937 made it illegal to fire a woman for being pregnant and provided her a small sum during her maternity leave. Child allowances, first undertaken in the same 1937 legislation, were paid directly to mothers, giving women "a real, though limited, influence on the financial situation of the family" (Ohlander 1991, 69). As evidenced by these efforts, Sweden "was a pioneer in the development of family law that assigned equal status to men and women" (Morgan 2006, 48).

In addition, World War II stimulated Sweden's economy, increasing the demand for female labor, both married and unmarried, in the industrial sector (Lundahl 2011, 163). While no country in Europe had a dual-earner or gender-equal regime in the 1940s, Sweden had a number of policies in place that supported women in employment outside the home. For instance, in 1925 the government passed a law granting women equal rights to men in civil service employment. The passage of this law began a pattern of support for female workers that was codified in 1938, in a law banning employment discrimination against married or pregnant women or single mothers. In addition, the solutions advocated in the Myrdals' book focused on reforms that would promote liberty and equality, particularly for women (Korsvold 2011, 141). Women played a strong role in the unions and Social Democratic party, which was critical for influencing the country's leadership to accept the right of women to work as a citizenship right (Hobson and Lindholm 1997; Sörensen and Bergqvist 2002). Thus, while still a male-breadwinner regime, by the early 1940s policy in Sweden was becoming oriented toward supporting women, married and single, in the workforce. All of these reforms in family and employment law supported, at least theoretically, the individuality and equality of women.

The material factor, Swedish agricultural policy, was set by experiences during World War I, when food policies that favored the importation of necessities resulted in shortages. During World War I, the government followed policies that allowed for the exportation of meat and animals to Germany, which was well received by farmers but less well received by urban residents. Despite this period of food shortages and a related distrust in government food policies, agricultural policies did not begin to truly change until the Great Depression, when a crisis agreement in 1933 between the Social Democrats and agrarian party created a guaranteed minimum price for milk (Martiin 2012, 159). This deal was the beginning of much more protectionist agricultural policies, which continued into World War II. As government officials were eager to avoid the mistakes of World War I, they created an array of policies during World War II that focused on encouraging production. These policies included price supports on a number of products, "compensation for harvest failure [and] ideas about income equality between farmers and factory workers" (Martiin 2012, 167). In addition to the system of price supports, the Swedish government was also determined to improve farmers' incomes. These principles governed Swedish agricultural policy until 1991 and reflected a state determined to enhance the welfare of all its citizens. The Swedish state clearly used agricultural policy in such a way as to encourage production.

The first suggestion for school meals at a state-funded level came in a 1900 Social Democratic party platform and was repeated in the 1911 platform. At that time, the party suggested free meals for poor children. It was not until 1935, following the publication of the Myrdals' book and the ascension of the Social Democrats to power, that the issue was brought up in a serious way. The 1935 Commission on Population Issues, on which Gunnar Myrdal served, released a report advocating free school lunch to improve the nutrition of the nation, but the government was not willing to fund the proposal at the time, in part due to the threat of World War II and the related buildup in defense measures. Following the war, as agricultural policies that encouraged production solidified and the country worked to encourage social equality, population health, and women's employment, a proposal for school lunches was revived and passed with the goal of giving women the opportunity to work and modernizing the nation through the rational investment in healthy children that would also encourage nutritious food consumption (Gullberg 2006). The promotion of population health, driven by the pro-natal block, was central to the creation of this policy, but the social understanding of women's roles played a part as well. School lunches were seen explicitly as a reform that enhanced gender equality and social equality (Gullberg 2006) as well as increased consumption of domestic agricultural products. In other words, ideational and material factors worked together to produce school lunches; Sweden provides a prime example of the way in which the presence of certain ideational factors make the creation of a meal program possible.

Norway

Norway provides an instructive counterpoint to Sweden: while it is also considered a social-democratic welfare state with an emphasis on universal programs that protect citizens against the market (Esping-Anderson 1990), it does not have a school lunch program. Norway had neither the agricultural production nor the gender ideology that supported women in outside employment. Instead, women in Norway were supported as mothers who were expected to be at home to care for their children. With the exception of dairy products, agriculture was primarily supported through direct income payments to farmers rather than through production incentives. Tracing the absence of these factors helps demonstrate their necessity to the creation of school lunches in Western Europe.

The lack of a school lunch in Norway is particularly surprising as the Oslo Breakfast, a cold meal of bread and cheese, was pioneered in Oslo in 1921 and became institutionalized as a large-scale feeding program in both Oslo and Bergen between 1931 and 1962. The substance of the meal itself, the *matpakken*, has become a cultural institution, eaten by everyone, but the provision of this meal by governmental agencies was purposefully discontinued in 1962. Historical institutionalism would suggest that these meals, or similar meals, would have continued due to the usual path dependence of such ingrained institutional arrangements (Pierson 2000; 2004). The purposeful discontinuance of the meals is a surprise, and the dual factors of agriculture and gender ideology account for this puzzle.

The contours of Norwegian agricultural policy were set in 1935, when the Farmer's Party cast its strength behind the Labour Party in exchange for deficiency payments, direct payments to farmers for the difference between the government-guaranteed price and the market price. This reflected the tangible interests of farmers in the Great Depression who wanted to assure themselves of guaranteed income. Further, the 1930 Joint Marketing Board created a system where farmers were given cash grants, in part to support themselves. The combination of these two systems, cash grants and deficiency payments, tend to discourage the overproduction of agricultural goods, leaving very little surplus food available in Norway for use in a school meal program.

However, even if there were not surplus goods, a country could still decide to create a school meal program and acquire food from elsewhere or change its agricultural policies in response to these demands. If there is demand for school meals, then governments might try to create them. However, in Norway there was no demand for school meals, largely due to a gender ideology that promoted women as caregivers, not earners. While Norwegian women gained several rights such as maternity leave and free assistance from midwives relatively early in the twentieth century, these measures worked to reinforce women in their central role as mothers and can be understood to strengthen the nuclear family (Sejersted 2011). Between 1919 and 1945, there was great debate in Norway over the role of women, and several policies resulted. Norway explicitly restricted married women's rights to work outside of the home beginning in 1925 during a period of high unemployment, a restriction that was not lifted until the late 1930s. A family allowance system was created in 1945 that reinforced women's role as caregivers (Seip and Ibsen 1991). Similarly, Norway has never created a public childcare system, like many of their neighbors, and instead continues to rely on private childcare with high religious content in the instruction (Sörenson 2011). The effect of these policies was to keep women out of the workforce and reduce demand for programs that might help women who were employed.

In fact, school meals were brought up several times in the Storting, the Norwegian parliament, between 1934 and 1945. In particular, the publication of the Myrdals' book was an important part of the political conversation in Norway, as well as Sweden, and forced Norwegian policy makers to seriously consider services in kind as advocated in the book. Unlike in Sweden, many labor party women argued against services in kind as they believed such services demonstrated a lack of confidence in mothers and poor and working-class families. Instead, these groups argued for cash to be transferred to mothers and families in the hopes that this would increase the general purchasing power of the country and produce better sales of agricultural goods.

In 1945, the Farmer's Party submitted a bill in Parliament that would have extended family allowances to cover all classes, as well as create a school meals program (*Stortingsforhandlinger* 1945–46). However, while the Labour Party was supportive of the notion of universality of the scheme, they were less supportive of services in kind, such as school meals. In the end, the debate over services in kind was won by the Labour Party, which held the majority and created the 1945 family allowances system

(*Stortingsforhandlinger* 1945–46), rejecting school meals and other service in kind programs. The Labour Party had already committed to extensive food subsidies in order to keep food prices low and was unwilling to create expensive new administrative schemes (Seip and Ibsen 1991). Further, women in Norway advocated for the food subsidies and the family allowance because these tools would help women in their role as caregivers. The objective, material interests of the Norwegian state following World War II were to increase economic production and the standard of living. While neighboring countries such as Sweden, facing the same material pressures, encouraged women to work (Sörenson 2011), Norway encouraged women to stay at home through a variety of policy measures or absences, including the lack of a school meal program.

In this case, the lack of a school lunch program is the result of political and cultural struggles in the 1930s and 1940s over the role of women and political deal making between the Labour and Farmer's parties in 1935. Both of these struggles resulted in policy choices that excluded women from the workforce and did not create agricultural surplus, institutionalizing the lack of demand and supply for a school lunch program. In particular, Norway had a historical gender ideology whereby women were conceived of as caregivers, not earners, and this ideology was reflected in policy choices that specifically kept women out of the workforce and reinforced their responsibility for feeding the family at home. While a number of policies were passed that affected women, these policies actively worked to keep women out of the workforce, rather than creating new possibilities for them. Gender ideology encouraged the creation of family allowances and discouraged the creation of a school lunch program. Ultimately, school meals were rejected due to the lack of any of the necessary material and ideational factors.

Germany

The lack of a school lunch program in Germany is perhaps not very surprising. They are considered a conservative welfare state, relying largely on the family to provide social services. And indeed, the German state has largely relied on families to provide meals to children throughout the day. However, Germany had the exact types of agricultural policy that have led to school meals in other states. Further, the German state did provide school meals during the two world wars but dismantled these programs in 1950. Despite the types of agricultural polices that led to the creation of school lunches elsewhere, in Germany the ideational component of gender, whereby women were expected to be at home in order to maintain and re-create German culture, as well as the desire to cement an individualist, democratic society, foreclosed the possibility of a school lunch program. Rather than demanding such programs, the collective voice explicitly militated against such programs.

Throughout the Nazi era, peasants were revered as an important cultural component of the German nation, and they were given guaranteed markets and prices for their goods. During World War II, the food situation in Germany was decent, due to the practice of exploiting both farmers in the occupied territories and German prisoners of war for their labor. However, following World War II and "the destruction of infrastructure and transportation networks, bad harvests, and a particularly cold winter of 1946–1947" (Gerhard 2012, 199), West German food policy began to focus on fixed prices and food rationing. Farmers were displeased with this new system, under which they received far less for their goods, and advocated in the late 1940s for subsidies and protection for farmers. Beginning in 1950, a wide-ranging price control system was set up on products including milk, bread, grain, cereals, meat, sugar, and fat, while import levies, taxes, and quotas were applied to protect farmers from competition (Gerhard 2012, 199). The memory of the hunger that followed World War II led the government to adopt polices that produced surpluses that the government held in reserve.

Although West Germany had the agricultural policy necessary for school meals, it did not create a meal program. The gender politics related to food in Germany were more decisive than any material factor. Germany was clearly a male-breadwinner state in the pre- and postwar period, creating policies that supported families by promoting male employment (Lewis 1992). Policies during the Nazi period were explicitly pro-father and designed to compensate men for doing their duty to the state by producing children (Bock 1991). Unlike Norway where the family allowance was given directly to the mother, in part to support and reinforce her in that role, in Nazi Germany family allowances were given to the father to in order to explicitly link economic rewards and fatherhood. This pattern continued in the postwar period as West Germany became entrenched as a male-breadwinner/female-homemaker state. This gender ideology had long roots that can be seen in the German school system. Half-day instruction, where children went to school in either the morning or afternoon, was introduced in areas of Prussian/German influence in 1872. It allowed the state to more effectively finance education, to avoid overburdening children with the rigors of schooling, and to ensure that children spent time at home with their families who were the ones expected to provide social and cultural education (Hagemann, Jarausch, and Allemann-Ghionda 2011). Of course, as fathers were expected to be working, the understanding was that it was mothers at home providing this social and cultural education. This was in contrast to England and France, for instance, where the schools were also expected to teach social and cultural norms. During the Weimar Republic, a movement emerged which advocated all-day schooling, based on the understanding that this would provide a more complete education; however, Christian-conservative opponents of this idea argued that such a move would, by allowing women to work outside the home, "destroy the family" (Hagemann 2011, 279). As such, half-day education remained the standard across what would become West Germany.

The pattern in East Germany was different, as women there were expected to work and school lunches were provided in order to more fully entrench the socialist model of the new state. In West Germany, the home-cooked meal "symbolized all that postwar Germans imagined that they had lost due to the war and occupation, and all they hoped to regain: familial integrity, physical and spiritual health, economic stability, and material well-being" (Weinreb 2011, 71). The role of women in providing that home-cooked meal became paramount to the state's task of re-envisioning itself as a capitalist society and preserving German culture and its traditional gender relationships. While the Western Allies had hoped to introduce all-day education, the state, both liberals and Christian-conservatives, firmly resisted this move, as it was seen as a threat to the centrality of the family (Hagemann 2011, 281). Even after World War II when West Germany, like most Western European states, experienced an economic boom and the concomitant need for labor, the state encouraged women into part-time rather than full-time work, specifically because it integrated well with their domestic duties (Hagemann, Jarausch, and Alleman-Ghionda 2011, 26). Further, despite the creation of school lunches in many democratic countries, in West Germany school meals were thought to threaten the notions of democracy and individualism so necessary for the new German state (Weinreb 2011).

In the German case, the ideational factor of gender, whereby women were expected to stay at home to care for their families, outweighed the material factor of agriculture, demonstrating that agriculture is a necessary but not sufficient condition for the creation of school lunch programs. The creation of these programs depends on the work of actors who explicitly connect ideas, in this case about women, to agricultural products.

Great Britain

Unlike the cases above, in Great Britain gender was not a determining factor in the creation of their school lunch program. Great Britain had very low rates of married women's employment and was not concerned, as Sweden was, with increasing those rates. Instead, against a familiar backdrop of agricultural policy and commitment to a welfare state, ideas about national security, as the country reeled from the Boer War and World War II, were the necessary ideational factors in this case.

In Great Britain school meals were legislated at two different times. The first was in 1906 when local education authorities were empowered to provide free or reduced-charge meals. While this legislation had the effect of increasing school meal uptake in some areas, it was not a universal system and required local effort to supply meals. In 1944, a national school meal act was passed that required local education authorities to provide meals and provided central government funding for the meals. Each of these two legislative acts was influenced by a war and security concerns. The 1906 act was passed directly following the Boer War, amid a collective worry about the fitness of British soldiers. The 1944 act was passed during World War II as the country began to look ahead to its postwar self. In this case, agricultural factors were necessary, but so too were ideational factors of security and a developing welfare state that sought to fundamentally reimagine the relationship between citizens and the state.

In Great Britain agriculture had been characterized by a laissez-faire approach since the repeal of the Corn Laws in 1846. The period between 1846 and 1931 saw Great Britain become dependent on food imports, which were allowed into the country without restriction. The British government was seemingly unconcerned with agricultural issues, worrying more about cheap food for consumers than either farmers' income or national self-sufficiency in foodstuffs (Short 2012, 172). Even with war approaching, the government hesitated to extend support to farmers, offering, in 1937, some help in purchasing fertilizer and extending subsidy payments from wheat to oats and barley. However, as Germany made its intentions clearer, the British government decided that creating a productivist agricultural system would be necessary in the face of war. Its decisions set the path for an intensively interventionist agricultural regime that had the explicit goals of increasing production and achieving self-sufficiency.

In 1939, the Defence of the Realm Act empowered the Ministry of Agriculture to control food production and agricultural land in order to maximize production, particularly of essential crops such as potatoes and wheat (Martin and Langthaler 2012, 57). The 1939 Agriculture Development Act further enshrined these goals by offering two pounds per acre for grassland converted to cereal production as well as more generous payments for oats and barley and extended payments for sheep (Short 2012, 173). While there are critiques to be made of the way this system forced small farmers who protested off their land and the way this system ushered in elements of a surveillance state (Martin and Langthaler 2012), the new agricultural regulations did increase production and ensured that the population did not suffer from hunger as compared to many other countries at the time (Ministry of Information 1946).

Following the success of the wartime controls on agriculture, the 1947 Agriculture Act enshrined high guaranteed prices for most agricultural products, creating a postwar agricultural system focused on increasing agricultural output, self-sufficiency, and farm incomes. The guaranteed price system was explicitly designed to encourage production by linking productivity to payments (Martin and Longthaler 2012). This policy was driven by a fear of backsliding into dependence on imports, fears of agriculture shortages that were impacting other countries in the late 1940s, and the obvious success of the wartime control system. Thus, Great Britain created a series of agricultural policies both during and immediately after the war that were designed to encourage production and overproduction. As such, Great Britain had the necessary factor of agricultural policy in place for the creation of a school lunch program. However, as the Germany case demonstrates, it is not enough to have agricultural products; actors must convince the government to use those products in a school meal program.

Like Germany, Great Britain is clearly classified as a male-breadwinner state, particularly in that time (Lewis 1992), relying on policies that support families only insofar as the husband was expected to be working and the mother at home taking care of the family. This model was supported by policies that restricted married women's ability to work outside the home during the interwar years such as a lack of maternity leave and state-supported childcare (Morgan 2006). William Beveridge, in the Beveridge Report, wrote explicitly about the importance of women as wives and mothers, an idea that was further codified in many of the Beveridgian welfare state policies (Lewis 1992). Because women's traditional roles in the home were so firmly entrenched in policy, Great Britain seems much like Germany and thus the creation of a school lunch program here is a surprise.

The fact that Great Britain created a school meal program, despite its strong male-breadwinner status, forces us to consider other factors. Educational time policies were one factor as the length of the British school day gradually became an all-day system, beginning in 1900, with morning and afternoon sessions and a break in the middle for lunch. The reason for the introduction of all-day schooling in England, in conjunction with compulsory education, was an attempt to control child labor in the factories (Hagemann, Jarausch, and Allemann-Ghionda 2011, 19). The first calls for a national meal program began when the compulsory education act was passed in 1876, with people arguing that if the law forced children to attend school, then some provision should be made for children to withstand the pressure of schooling. As early as 1883 the *Lancet* weighed in on the debate, arguing, "That good feeding is necessary for brain nutrition does not need to be demonstrated or even argued at length. It is cruel to educate a growing child unless you are also prepared to feed him." Thus, the creation of compulsory education and the gradual development of the all-day school created awareness of the issue of feeding children—although at the time most feeding was either done at home by mothers or by welfare organizations—and also created a school system amenable to the introduction of school meals by virtue of this schedule.

While a number of child welfare reformers had been campaigning for school meals since the mid-1860s (Bulkley 1914, 3), school feeding became a potent national issue in 1902 following an army report that three out of every five men seeking to enlist in the army during the Boer War (1898–1902) were found to be physically unfit due to improper nutrition.[3] "The quality of the recruits was so dire that the height requirement for the infantry was reduced" (Davies 2005). This report caused considerable public alarm, and a Labour Party pamphlet from 1905 states that "there is no need to dwell upon our lowered standards for recruits or our physical, mental and moral ineptitude in South Africa, the full degradation of which has only dawned on us by comparison with the Japanese in war and in victory. The nation is awake to the danger of physical degeneration at last" (Clark 1948).

Based on these concerns with fitness and the implications for national security, a number of organizations were created, including the Inter-Departmental Committee on Physical Deterioration, and they spoke strongly about the need for the state to take a role in feeding children (Webster 1993). These pressures resulted in the passage of the Education (Provision of Meals) Bill on December 21, 1906, to fund school meals through local education authorities.[4] This law only allowed schools to provide meals when the local education authorities thought it was in the best interest of the children, when they had the money to do so, and when voluntary agencies had failed at the task. Due to this, the adoption of the act was gradual. It was not until the beginning of World War II that national school meals legislation was seriously considered. National school meals legislation, introduced by the Labour Party in 1937, was defeated (*The Times* 1937), but the beginning of World War II produced a steady drumbeat of proclamations about school meals from government officials. The war brought school meals more forcefully into the nation's consciousness: "with the outbreak of the Second World War, raising the standards of the nation's health was recognised as an essential prerequisite for maintaining morale" (Gillard 2003). During the second world war, it became apparent that school meals as they were, especially under the constraints of rationing, were failing children; one of the greatest concerns was that rationing was disproportionately affecting schoolchildren, as their nutritional needs were different from the needs of adults.

In Great Britain, the link between malnutrition and security was made evident in the Boer War and was built upon by the efforts of Lord Woolton in World War II. Lord Woolton, the minister of food from 1940 to 1943 and the minister of reconstruction beginning in 1943, declared himself committed to feeding children (*The Times* 1941a) and actively campaigned for school meals as a wartime necessity and future security measure (*The Times* 1943; *The Times* 1941c). In addition to support from Lord Woolton, *The Times* itself declared school meals a wartime necessity, echoing some of the arguments from the conversations after the Boer War (*The Times* 1941b).

This editorial declaration raised a flurry of responses both for and against school meals. While some argued against school meals, largely on the basis that the provision of meals would decrease individual responsibility (*The Times* 1941d), the majority of letter writers spoke in favor of school meals, suggesting that during the war, the need of national fitness was greater than before and that school meals could contribute to meeting this need (*The Times* 1941e).

In addition, the school meal program was one part of the larger welfare state that was being created in Great Britain at that time. The Beveridge Report (1942) set broad goals for the British welfare state of comprehensive social security, including full employment, free health service, and family allowances (Abel-Smith 1992).While many of the goals were never fully realized, the report presented a new vision of society that included the idea that governments should organize the economic resources of their state in the interests of the people in the state and according to the concept of "freedom from want," that governments should take responsibility for the welfare of their people (Beveridge 1942). The school meal program was part of this larger vision of a new society. Indeed, the school meal program that emerged was a universalist, national system, adhering closely to the welfare state approach that appeared in numerous other issues areas following the war in Great Britain.

The 1944 Education Act was a revolutionary act that laid out a new vision for British education and worked to remove inequities in the education system. This act required every local education authority to provide a meal to any child who wanted one. While the program did not reach to every district in the country until 1965, it was fully funded by 1947. This commitment to the program reflects the way in which ideational concerns with security and the welfare state worked with agricultural policy to produce a school lunch program. Gender does not figure prominently in this case, unlike in some of the other countries examined here; in Britain the material availability of agricultural products were forcefully linked to concerns such as child malnutrition to provide the impetus for a school lunch program.

WESTERN EUROPE VERSUS THE UNITED STATES

Each country in Western Europe had its own particular developmental track as it created or did not create a school meals program in the 1930s and 1940s. In some countries gender regime was a determining factor, while in others a more complicated interaction between agricultural policy, educational policy, new ideas about government's relationship to its citizenry, and national security existed. In each country, the way in which the various factors interacted was different and was time dependent: some states created programs before the war to respond to the Great Depression, while others created programs after the war as they created new welfare states or as concerns with national security dominated their policy making. In all cases, the creation of a meal program depended on the ability of actors to recognize the possibilities presented by the material factor of agricultural policy and advocate for school meal programs using the ideas that resonated best in their particular national context.

In this early phase, a number of ideas were concerns to society as a whole and actors working to improve child nutrition had to find the right frame onto which to harness their concerns. The next chapter examines the creation of the program in the United States, where security concerns dominated the national conversation and shaped policy makers' and advocates' ability to respond to agricultural surpluses and child malnutrition. While a concern with gender was important in many of the European countries, gender was less important for the creation of the National School Lunch Program in the United States and the subsequent impact of the United States on spreading this program model around the world through the work of the World Food Programme.

4 · THE UNITED STATES

Surplus, Security, and Schools

In the United States, a national program was instituted in 1946 that is the largest program in terms of number of children fed in the developed world today. This political and institutional development is surprising when one considers other United States welfare programs. The system created by the United States is commonly considered a liberal welfare state, meaning that the state prefers private social benefits and offers only residual public protections, usually based on means testing (Esping-Anderson 1990; Morgan 2006; Titmuss 1958). In terms of childcare, the usual measure of a state's responsiveness to both women and children, the United States offers very little programming and depends almost entirely on the private market to provide solutions to that welfare issue (O'Connor, Orloff, and Shaver 1999; Morgan 2006; Sainsbury 1999). Generally speaking, the United States has only a limited or reluctant child and family policy (Gauthier 1996, 6). And yet, the United States has created and maintained a feeding program for children that is, for the most part, supported by the state and administered by the state. In addition, while there is means testing for some children to receive free or reduced-rate lunch, all children can partake in a heavily subsidized, cheap meal.

The school lunch program was created out of a process of contestation that involved southern Democrats, child welfare reformers, nutritionists, and the military serving their entrenched interests. However, what is often overlooked in analyses of the creation of the school lunch program is the way in which ideas, in particular about charity, nutrition, and security, were used by these actors to further their particular causes. The historical formation of the school lunch program in the United States depended on the ability of policy entrepreneurs to link the economic concerns of agricultural production with the ideational concern of national security, which was culturally resonant as the country emerged from World War II. The United States created a school lunch program due to the explicit interaction between ideational and material factors, as security concerns built on agricultural surpluses. This is different from Canada, which did not create a program, despite similar agricultural policies and gender ideology. As in the European cases, it is useful to compare countries that share many similarities and yet reached different conclusions in the creation of this particular policy, as it highlights the importance of ideational factors in policy creation.

NUTRITION, AGRICULTURE, AND WAR

Experimentation with school lunches first started at the local level and only slowly moved up to the state and then federal level. The first forty years of the twentieth century witnessed cities struggling with the issue of feeding schoolchildren in the face of poverty, and school lunches became a locus for debates over the role of charity, the family, and the American work ethic. It was only due to the agricultural policies instituted during the Great Depression and the security concerns raised by World War II that the federal government became compelled to feed children. The war gave policy advocates a new language with which to discuss school lunches, and they were able to successfully argue that school lunches were a security measure for the good of the country.

The first feeding program in the United States was at the Children's Aid Society of New York, which instituted a school feeding program for its vocational school in 1855. Other organizations were slow to follow: it was not until the turn of the century that more private societies and associations interested in children's welfare and education became concerned about children who could not afford a lunch. In particular, at the beginning of the twentieth century, nutritionists, physicians, teachers, and home economists began to see school lunch programs as a vehicle for promoting the new scientific methods of eating and nutrition. While nutrition science had improved rapidly in the early years of the twentieth century, including the discovery of vitamins, the proponents of nutrition science had been unable to convince people to take advantage of nutritious eating, probably in part to their moralizing and missionary fervor, which led them to speak with an alienating and judgmental tone (Levine 2008, 22). Ellen Richards, a home economics pioneer, developed large-scale industrial kitchens that could serve nutritionally sound meals backed by the scientific principles of rationality, efficiency, and standardization. Richards's first kitchen was in a working-class neighborhood in Boston, but it closed after three years due to lack of customers, and then she also modeled this kitchen at the Chicago World's Fair in 1893. After the close of the fair, Richards realized that school lunchrooms were "the perfect system for bringing nutrition to a wide public" (Levine 2008, 22). Richards and others believed that schools would be able to both provide food based on nutrition science and teach about proper nutrition, as the students would take the lessons from their meals home with them; adherents to the Richard's model believed that the inculcation of nutritional values through school lunches would be more likely to succeed in changing societal perceptions of healthy eating than the previous moralizing and missionary efforts of home economists and nutritionists.

In addition to the work of nutritionists, the publication of Robert Hunter's *Poverty: Social Conscience in a Progressive Era* in 1904 and John Spargo's *The Bitter Cry of Children* in 1906 increased concerns about hungry children in schools. Hunter was a social reformer in Chicago who traveled in the same circles as Jane Addams and lived for a while in the Toynbee Hall settlement in England, where he became more aware of social problems. Spargo was a British socialist who organized the Labour Parliamentary Representation Committee, a forerunner of the Labour Party, before coming to the United States in 1901.

Both of these books focused on the alarming numbers of hungry children and included some of the rudimentary science regarding the effects of the lack of food on learning. Spargo estimated that "not less than 2,000,000 children of school age in the United States are the victims of poverty which denies them common necessities, particularly adequate nourishment" (Spargo 1906, 117). Hunter, who wrote the introduction for Spargo's book, focused on the link between food and learning, writing, "Few of us sufficiently realize the powerful effect upon life of adequate food. Few of us ever think how much it is responsible for our physical and mental advancement or what a force it has been in forwarding our civilized life" (Spargo 1906). The links between food and brain function had already been written about in Great Britain, as far back as 1883 (*Lancet* 1883). While those already serving lunches in the United States had also made these connections, the publication of these two books helped to draw attention to this understanding and concern. These books were part of a growing international debate on the health and welfare of children (Cunningham 2005).

Following the publication of these two books, several large cities in the United States began instituting school feeding. Poverty advocates were able to use the arguments in the books to push for the creation of school lunch programs. Most of these efforts occurred first through various voluntary agencies, but they were taken over by school boards as the programs grew in size. By 1920, feeding programs were in place in Philadelphia, Boston, Milwaukee, New York, Cleveland, Cincinnati, St. Louis, Chicago, and Los Angeles. Chicago and Los Angeles had the most substantial programs at this time as the programs had been implemented in both the high schools and the elementary schools. Both of these cities' programs were sponsored by their boards of education but operated on a concession basis. These were not free meals but self-supporting meal programs.

This development was not without controversy (*Chicago Daily Tribune* 1921a; 1921b). Generally, concessionaire service resulted in lower-quality foods, and those concerned with appropriate nutrition argued for city service. While the price for the meals was standard across the concessionaires, the supplies were chosen by the concessionaires, who could choose to purchase lesser-quality foods. Chicago seems to have struggled with the issue of concessionaire service more than other cities. In 1902 students railed against the quality of the concessionaire's food at one high school while students at a different high school received highly acclaimed food, all for the same price (*Chicago Daily Tribune* 1902). In 1916 an experimental program, whereby the household science departments of each school ran the school lunches, was declared successful, and the school board began to look into the possibility of removing concessionaire service totally. The principals of the schools not participating in the program were "anxious [that] the lunchrooms be placed under the management of the household science department because of the profit, the decreased cost of lunch to pupils and the educational value to the girls taking household science" (*Chicago Daily Tribune* 1916).

However, after five years of management by household science departments, the Chicago Board of Education turned lunch service back to concession companies in 1921 in an attempt to cuts costs, which resulted in protests by many students (*Chicago Daily Tribune* 1921a). The complaints were largely about the quality of the food and included comments such as "The cauliflower has been warmed up since Monday, becoming sour yesterday," "Lamb croquettes have a strong liver taste," and "A charge of one cent is made for half cubes of sugar" (*Chicago Daily Tribune* 1921a). The Women's City Club of Chicago added its two cents to the debate by writing an angry letter to the Board of Education decrying the commercialization of school lunches and worrying that this would exploit and be detrimental to the health of schoolchildren (*Chicago Daily Tribune* 1921b).

Not all school districts experimented with concessionaire service, and in those that did not, there was a push by the voluntary agencies that operated feeding programs to convince school boards to take more control over the lunches. This contestation played out in different ways in different cities. For instance, in 1909, in Philadelphia, the Starr Center Association's operations in the high schools were transitioned to the Philadelphia school board for one year as an experiment. The Starr Center Association was a local cooperative community service organization focused on "the educational and social improvement of the poor neighborhoods" (Starr Center Association of Philadelphia, Records 1894–1973). The Starr Center's experiment proved so successful in terms of low cost and healthy food that the School Lunch Committee of the Home and School League, which had been serving lunches in the elementary schools, asked the board to take over its program in 1915 (Smedley 1930, 15). The transition between voluntary agencies and the school board took six years and was accomplished with little hesitation on either side.

In New York, on the other hand, a transition took twelve years and followed several years of high-profile lobbying on the part of various interest groups. The first school lunches in New York were provided in 1908, when a Principal Chatfield of Public School 51 asked permission of the Board of Education to provide school lunches, with the assurance that it would not cost the board anything. Dr. William Maxwell, superintendent of the New York schools, had been urging school lunches and readily agreed to the plan. After receiving permission, Principal Chatfield formed the New York School Lunch Committee, which operated as a local voluntary organization. The lunches served by the New York School Lunch Committee cost three cents and included "soup, salad or nourishing vegetable, bread, and a dessert" (*New York Times* 1913). In addition, the committee worked hard to ensure that children were given foodstuffs of their ethnic background, such as kosher food for Jewish children or lima beans and macaroni for Italian children (*New York Times* 1913). By 1913, the New York School Lunch Committee was serving lunches in seven schools, but eighty more schools were asking for the lunches. The New York School Lunch Committee informed the school board that it could not meet the demand and the Board of Education must take over the lunches.

However, it was not until 1920 that the Board of Education began to run the lunch service. Lunches in the meantime continued to be supplied by the New York School Lunch Committee, which extended its work to thirty schools by 1918 (*New York Times* 1918a). Beginning in 1918, lobbying began for the board of education to provide school lunches and included pleas by socialist members of the board of aldermen, the board of health, and various medical and educational interests (*New York Times* 1918b; 1918c; 1918d). These pleas were finally heeded when, in 1920, the Board of Education took over operating forty-four lunchrooms that had previously been operated by voluntary organizations such as the New York School Lunch Committee.

In the United States, resistance to school boards taking responsibility for school lunches was largely a debate about the roles of the state and the family. For instance, in Milwaukee, the school board refused to take over school feeding from the Women's School Alliance of Wisconsin out of fear that such an act would encourage parental irresponsibility (Gunderson 1971, 7). While the state had become concerned with the issue of infant mortality and children's health in the 1910s, the national government's support for families was limited, largely believing that the issue should be solved by the market or charities (Gauthier 1996). This national reluctance for a coherent or explicit child and family policy was reflected at the local level as individual polities wrestled with the issue of child malnutrition.

The work of children's welfare advocates, nutritionists, and home economists to cement the idea that government-provided school lunches would benefit the nation by creating healthier children with better manners was essential to the eventual creation of school lunch programs. They provided a strong argument for state intervention into the daily lives of children and families, and their work was an important part of the progressive reform movement's efforts to expand progressive-era victories that had occurred during World War I. A nutrition-oriented understanding of the issue suggested one important reason that the state should take responsibility for feeding children: it would "enhanc[e] the health of the entire nation" (Levine 2008, 38). However, the federal government would need a push from other quarters to become fully convinced that it bore responsibility in this case.

THE ROLE OF U.S. AGRICULTURE

Despite the efforts of the nutritionists, support for school lunches dwindled throughout the 1920s across the country (*New York Times* 1927). In New York, support by the Board of Education for school lunches dwindled from a high of forty-four lunchrooms to twenty-seven, and concessionaries began taking over the other lunchrooms (*New York Times* 1927). This resulted in angry outcries from those concerned with the issue, particularly regarding quality of the food. In Chicago, on the other hand, an article urged mothers to take advantage of the healthy school lunches rather than send their children to school with pantry leftovers with little nutritive value (*Chicago Daily Tribune* 1925).

While funding and supplies for school lunches dwindled, the beginning of the Great Depression intensified concern about the malnourishment of schoolchildren and the plight of farmers. States began to pass laws authorizing school boards to operate lunchrooms,[1] but a lack of money hindered these efforts. At a local level, relief fund organizations were created to provide lunches for school children. The *Chicago Daily Tribune* created the Hungry Children's Fund and published contributors to the fund on a regular basis. While the Chicago fund depended on individual contributors, the New York City School Relief Fund automatically deducted funds from teachers' salaries to contribute to the fund, which displeased the teachers' union (*New York Times* 1932). As the Depression continued, teacher salaries were reduced, resulting in a reduction in available contributions.

At the same time, the Great Depression was causing hardship for American farmers. In the 1920s, many of them had rapidly industrialized, but with the market crash these industrial techniques resulted in massive overproduction of many agricultural staples. The U.S. government's initial reaction was to destroy crops and animals. For instance, in 1933 the Corn-Hog program was announced by Secretary of Agriculture Henry Wallace, which aimed to remove pigs from the market by offering high prices for small pigs and then turning these pigs into "fertilizer, hog feed, and meat for the poor," with the vast majority of them being turned into fertilizer (Winders 2009, 52). Only 20 percent of the purchased pigs were distributed to hungry citizens (White 2015). Likewise, other crops were plowed under or dumped. While some products were used for the hungry, most were simply removed from the market, partly out of a fear that governmental relief for the hungry would reduce the American work ethic. These disposal programs angered the American public, and protests by both consumers and farmers broke out across the country (White 2015).

The Corn-Hog program emerged out of the Agricultural Adjustment Act (AAA) of 1933. This act was an integral part of the New Deal and shared the goal of other New Deal programs of alleviating the Depression through government action. It was designed to create a more sustainable agricultural system and sought to raise the price of agricultural goods by restricting production. Essentially, the AAA worked as a supply management system by creating a price support system. Despite the goal of restricting production, these price supports instead created incentives for farmers to overproduce farm commodities (Winders 2009). Schoolchildren became a ready outlet for these surplus commodities.

In searching for a way to dampen consumer protest over the Corn-Hog program but preserve the outlines of supply management, the group of agricultural economists that came up with the Corn-Hog program eventually came up with the idea to send the surpluses to schoolchildren (Levine 2008, 46). Following the advice of this group, in 1933 Secretary Wallace began to use the Federal Surplus Commodities Corporation (FSCC)[2] to distribute surpluses to the needy and in particular began distributing surplus foods such as dairy, pork, and wheat to schools. This accomplished the dual goals of removing certain products from the market while distributing them to the needy, and thus provided a counter-narrative to consumer protests against the government's food policy.

Due to the incentives of the Agricultural Adjustment Act, farm surpluses continued to build over the next three years. In 1936, Congress passed Public Law 320 in order to help both children and farmers. PL 320 gave the secretary of agriculture monies "equal to 30 percent of the gross receipts from duties collected under the custom laws during the calendar year" (Gunderson 1971, 13). This money was to be used to remove surplus foods from the market, which were continuing to depress prices, and dispose of them in such a way as to not interfere with normal sales. The law solidified the practices put into place in 1933. By 1939, PL 320 was helping 14,075 schools and 892,259 schoolchildren receive surplus commodities, with the FSCC hoping to reach 5 million children by 1940 (*New York Times* 1939). In addition, the FSCC worked specifically with state and local authorities, PTAs, and other voluntary organizations to ensure the expansion of school lunch programs. At this point economic concerns, more than any arguments about child malnutrition, helped ensure that children were fed. Even as the Depression lessened in intensity, the number of children being fed through these programs continued to increase due to pressure from agricultural producers and the surpluses that were created by Depression policies.

PL 320 and the Agricultural Adjustment Act of 1933 solidified the American agricultural welfare state that had begun in the second half of the nineteenth century with the creation of the USDA, the land-grant college system, and state agricultural experimental stations (Sheingate 2003). The agricultural welfare state, characterized by government intervention into agricultural markets, set the stage for the creation of school lunch programs as these pieces of legislation regulated the production and consumption of food (Sheingate 2003). The basic infrastructure of the National School Lunch Program was created at that time and reflects the premise of the American agricultural welfare state. For instance, in order to receive food, schools had to sign an agreement promising:

- that the commodities would not be sold or exchanged
- that the food purchases would not be discontinued or curtailed because of the receipt of surplus foods
- that the program would not be operated for profit. (Gunderson 1971, 14)

In addition, commodities then and now are allotted based on a maximum quantity of foodstuff per child, as calculated by the USDA. For some commodities, there is no maximum. These rules highlight the primary goal of supporting agriculture for the school lunch program in the face of farm surpluses in the 1930s.

In addition to providing food and dealing with the agricultural surplus problem, the federal government used the school lunch program to put people to work. The Works Progress Administration (WPA) provided work for needy persons and, through the Community Service Division of the WPA, placed many unemployed women in school lunch programs as cooks, servers, bakers, clerks, and typists. This combination of agricultural surpluses and a ready and cheap workforce resulted in the rapid expansion of school lunch programs across the country. By February 1942, school lunch programs were in operation in every state and provided federal assistance to 92,916 schools that served 6 million children daily.

WAR

The National School Lunch Program could be seen as the result of a path-dependent process whereby programs created under the auspices of charity or better nutrition naturally led to a national program. In addition, the agricultural subsidy formulas that had been put in place during the Great Depression contributed to the formation of the national program, as lawmakers from agricultural states lobbied aggressively for a program that would allow for the continuation of these subsidies. These two factors might make for a standard historical institutionalist argument about the creation of this program. However, despite the importance of path dependence for understanding the emergence of the program, it was the war itself that was essential for the creation of the school meals program, as it provided an opportunity for a diverse group of policy entrepreneurs to refocus the national conversation on the connection between security and child malnutrition. It is unlikely that the path dependence of previous programs would have been strong enough to break the federal government's natural reluctance to take on issues of family and child welfare, as evidenced through the

United States' lack of a comprehensive family and child policy, without the critical juncture of World War II.

World War II demonstrated a connection between national fitness, security, and child malnutrition in the United States in a way similar to the Boer War in the United Kingdom forty years earlier. In addition, a concern with women's employment and their ability to provide meals for their children served to bring attention to a school lunch program. Thus, within a political and economic context of existing limited lunch programs and existing agricultural subsidy programs, teachers, women's advocates, supporters of agriculture, and children's advocates reached out to use the language of security that was readily available due to the end of World War II. They were able to use this language and frame child malnourishment as a national security issue.

World War II changed existing lunch programs; as more people found work in the defense industries the WPA was eliminated, and farm surpluses were diverted toward the armed forces. The quantity of food available for school lunches dropped "from a high of 454 million pounds in 1942 to 93 million pounds by 1944" (Gunderson 1971, 16); the subsidized food was now going to soldiers. Due to this, by 1944 the school lunch program had shrunk to 34,064 schools. However, this drop was temporary, and by 1945 the numbers had rebounded. This was partly because Congress took it upon itself to maintain the school lunch program at least somewhat by passing legislation during the war years that provided cash subsidy payments for the purchase of food for school lunches to the tune of $50 million per year. However, funding was often uncertain, and school districts that had made school lunch plans with the expectation of certain amounts of money were often disappointed (*New York Times* 1943a). In addition, this year-to-year legislation meant that schools were uncertain if they would receive federal aid in the future and were thus reluctant to take on the tasks of building kitchens and installing expensive kitchen equipment.

During the later war years, arguments against continuing federal aid were largely based on "the contention that these plans utilized surplus foods and that there is now no surplus foods to be distributed" (*New York Times* 1943a). Supporters argued that providing food should be part of a national security policy. This argument had been aired initially during World War I, when Dr. Henry Dwight Chapman, head of the children's department of the Post-Graduate Hospital, argued in several speeches and letters to the editor that "children form the great second line of defense in future trouble" and that all must be done to "secure their normal development" (*New York Times* 1918a). He saw school lunch programs as a security measure, and this justification was taken up by progressive-era reformers focused on improving nutrition. This line of thinking received a great boost after an investigation into the health of young men rejected in the World War II draft showed physical deficiencies that were due to childhood malnutrition, similar to what had occurred in Great Britain following the Boer War.

Schools and women's organizations began to argue that school lunches should be considered wartime policy. The entry of women into the workforce during the war spurred women's organizations to call for school lunches (McLaughlin 1943; *New York Times* 1943b; Oppenheim 1943). Some estimated that as many as half the women in the United States had entered the workforce during the war, and it was difficult for them to come home at noon and prepare a lunch. In addition, rationing affected the sorts of foods that were available for lunches at home. The assistant superintendent for New York City schools spoke of this factor when he observed that "rationing had thrown women off their stride" (Levine 2008, 57). Others working on the issue insisted simply that working mothers did not have the time to create properly balanced lunches for their children (Levine 2008, 57). The war created working mothers as a constituency supportive of school lunches. Women's employment during the war was certainly one of the factors that went into increasing school lunch coverage, although not the primary factor.

The congressional call for a permanent school lunch program came from a conservative Democratic senator from Georgia, Richard Russell. Russell thought poorly of most social welfare legislation, but he was from an agricultural state and supported any effort to help his constituents (Levine 2008, 76). In pressing for national school lunch legislation, he said, "The school lunch program has proven exceptional benefit to the children, schools, and agriculture of the country as a whole" (House Committee on Agriculture 1946). Agricultural interests were cemented into the program.

As legislators like Russell began lobbying for a more permanent program in order to encourage food production and consumption (Levine 2008, 76), it was determined that the aid that had been operating for the past ten years had been useful to both children and the agricultural industries and that permanent legislation should be passed (House of Representatives 1945).

Some saw the creation of the national program as inevitable. However, there was pushback from a number of quarters, primarily from those concerned about increasing the role of the national government, reducing the responsibility of parents, or creating socialism (*Congressional Record* 1946a).

Despite these concerns, the House reports make clear that the primary focus of the legislation was to cement agricultural production and consumption in place as the war came to a close, and that the pro-school-lunches legislators regarded the war as an opportunity to create permanent legislation supporting farmers. For instance, the majority of the reports on the school lunch program come from the House Committee on Agriculture and stress "the agricultural nature of the program" while seeing the child welfare features of the program as an unexpected benefit for the defense of the nation (U.S. Senate 1945). Here the link between security and the school lunch program is made explicit. Likewise, John Flanagan, a Virginia representative and cosponsor of the legislation, explicitly argued that feeding children was necessary for national defense (*Congressional Record* 1946a, 1454). These reports argue that education and child care are the proper domain of the individual states but "that the National Government, insofar as it has a direct interest in the maintenance of farm income and in a healthy citizenry, should use its resources to encourage the States in the work" (U.S. Senate 1945).Those members of Congress focused on agriculture took advantage of the window provided by World War II to solidify agricultural subsidies that continue today, by emphasizing the creation of healthy students for future defense purposes.

Interestingly, while the hearings were held in the agricultural committees and representatives from the Department of Agriculture, the War Food Administration, and the National Farmers Union were present, there were also representatives from a variety of other organizations (House Committee on Agriculture Hearings 1945; House Committee on Appropriations 1945; U.S. Senate Committee on Agriculture and Forestry Hearings 1944). This list includes women's organizations such as the General Federation of Women's Clubs, the Congress of Women's Auxiliaries, and the American Association of University Women. Educational organizations included the National Council of Chief State School Officers, the National Education Association, the Connecticut Department of Education, the Association for Childhood Education, and the National Congress of Parents and Teachers. The United Automobile Workers and the CIO had representatives there, as well as the American Home Economics Association. Finally, a number of directors of school lunch programs were also there. A diverse number of interest groups came together to testify for this program, providing evidence of the number of groups that stood to benefit from a positive decision.

In 1946, the House Committee on Agriculture advised that for the benefit of children, schools, and agriculture, the school lunch program should be made a permanent part of school systems and that the education features of a properly chosen diet should be emphasized. The Senate Committee on Agriculture and Forestry passed a bill as well, although with differences in the amount of initial funding. Once these differences were resolved, largely in favor of the Senate's more generous version, the National School Lunch Act of 1946 was passed. The language of the legislation reflects the concerns mentioned above, stressing the importance of agriculture, national security, and the role of the state: "As a measure of national security, to safeguard the health and well-being of the Nation's children and to encourage the domestic consumption of nutritious agricultural commodities and other food, by assisting the States, through grants in aid and other means, in providing an adequate supply of food and other facilities for the establishment, maintenance, operation and expansion of nonprofit school lunch programs" (House of Representatives 1946). This language remains today in the School Lunch Act that is passed every five years. Clearly, both security and agricultural concerns were important to the creation of the program, as well as its continuation. In fact, it is likely that the bill would not have emerged if these twin concerns had not been taken advantage of by policy entrepreneurs interested in a permanent school lunch program. These entrepreneurs included a wide variety of actors, including those concerned with child malnutrition and those concerned with meeting the needs of agricultural producers who stressed the connection between school meals and security.

Evidence for the centrality of the idea of security to the creation of the National School Lunch Program comes from the way in which defenders of the program spoke about it in various committee hearings. Secretary Wallace and Rep. Flanagan both flagged the importance of the school lunch program as a guard against communism and Nazism (*Congressional Record* 1946b, 1611; *Congressional Record* 1956, 1454), and statements made in the public hearings connected the lunch program to national security (*New York Times* 1944). President Harry Truman when he signed the bill highlighted the utility of the program in strengthening the nation (*New York Times* 1946). The language of the bill itself highlights national security as one of the goals of the program. Although agricultural interests were at stake, supporters of the national school lunch program were able to use worries about national security and the connection between nutrition and fitness for army service to make a compelling argument with national resonance.[3]

The momentous events of World War II gave a variety of policy makers the opening to push for a variety of social changes, including the welfare state in general and school lunch programs in particular. The war gave policy entrepreneurs the chance to reframe child malnourishment in the resonant discourse of that moment: security. By declaring unfed children to be a security issue, feeding children necessitates more invasive kinds of state intervention because "the special nature of security threats justifies the use of extraordinary measures to handle them" (Buzan, Waever, and de Wilde 1998, 21), including massive new social programs. Policy entrepreneurs used the concerns of security to argue that feeding programs were necessary for the future security of the country, as children would become the soldiers of the future.

However, it is unlikely that the war alone would have provided enough of an opportunity for policy entrepreneurs to push for a national school meal program if the groundwork had not already been laid for the connection between agricultural subsidies and schools. The role of agricultural interests is of utmost importance for understanding the emergence of the school lunch program in the United States. If the infrastructure of agricultural subsidies and school lunches as commodity dumping grounds had not been created during the Depression, it is unlikely that school lunches would have emerged as national policy. The development of agricultural subsidies was an important precursor, as the material supplies were available. However, it was the explicit connection that actors made in the public arena between schools, security, and surpluses that resulted in the national school lunch program.

The National School Lunch Program was created due to both material and ideational factors. In this case, choices made by the government as to how to support agriculture during the Great Depression resulted in surpluses and subsidies that farmers were eager to continue. The fear created by the World War II about national security allowed those invested in child malnutrition and agriculture to press for a school meal program in order to solve the twin problems of these surpluses and this future insecurity. The entrepreneurs' ability to use a relevant and resonant idea was key to completing the historical process of creating a national school lunch program in the United States.

CANADA

In Canada there is no national school lunch program, although in the last fifteen years piecemeal efforts have sprung up to provide meals to some children living in poverty. Compared to the United States it is surprising to realize that Canada does not have a school lunch program, due to its relatively advanced welfare state apparatus. Like the United Kingdom and the United States, Canada is commonly considered a "liberal" welfare state according to Esping-Anderson's classifications, and both the United States and United Kingdom have national school lunch programs. These two countries developed their welfares states at similar times and under similar circumstances as Canada, and thus the omission of lunches in Canada is puzzling. Much like in Norway and Germany, additional ideational factors were in play, namely a restrictive gender ideology that precluded a government lunch program. Because of the way in which the gender ideology closed off the possibilities for a lunch program, this comparison also highlights the importance of actors who are able to take advantage of strategic political moments.

Canada's agricultural policy, although driven by a different history, looked very similar to that of the United States both during the Great Depression and following World War II. The government supported agricultural producers through price support policies that resulted in large surpluses, particularly of wheat. Canada's agricultural policy was set in place by the events of World War I, when wheat supplies in particular were threatened, leading to the creation of the Board of Grain Supervisors, with the goal of stabilizing wheat prices and supplies. Federal control was ceded during the 1920s to prairie wheat pools that used cooperative principles to control wheat prices and supply in order to ensure stable incomes for farmers. While this cooperative pooling effort was initially successful, such that Canada supplied almost a third of the world's wheat exports, market disasters with the onset of the Great Depression threatened the livelihood of the western provinces (Way 2013). In the early 1930s, the federal government once again stepped in to help the western provinces and established the Canadian Wheat Board as a voluntary marketing mechanism in 1935 (Menzies 1973).

In 1943, it became compulsory for farmers to sell to the Canadian Wheat Board in order to have a stable supply during the war. Farmers were provided with an elaborate system of subsidies to hold down prices, and the government committed itself to provide support for farmers after the war. The Canadian Federation of Agriculture urged the government to provide a price floor after the war, since it had enforced a price ceiling during the war (Britnell and Fowke 1962). Parliament passed the Agricultural Prices Support Act in 1944 as a provisional measure, which was made permanent in 1950. The act created a board that had the goal of price stabilization through either outright purchases or deficiency payments. The board preferred outright purchases in instances where commodity-specific marketing boards did not already exist; in those cases they used deficiency payments. As such, and as we have seen in other countries, these policies led to the creation of a large surpluses, particularly in wheat. In fact, surpluses were explicitly encouraged under the 1946 Anglo-Canadian Wheat Agreement, which was designed to provide a steady supply and price assurance to the United Kingdom and price assurance to Canadian wheat producers.

From the end of World War II until 1970, the Canadian government actively pursued a policy of surplus agriculture, particularly in grains, even rejecting deficiency payments when they were suggested in the 1950s. There was a belief that these policies were right and the surpluses inevitable (Menzies 1973). However, there was never any suggestion that these surpluses be used to alleviate domestic poverty. Instead, the surpluses were either destined for export or developing countries, and the government accepted that some product would simply remain in government storage. While the same agricultural policies and buildup in the United States was channeled into domestic feeding programs, in particular the National School Lunch Program, this was never suggested in Canada.

Certainly part of the reason why policy took this direction lies in the fact that protests such as those over the Corn-Hog program in the United States never erupted in Canada; there was not pressure on the Canadian government to funnel surpluses toward domestic programs as there was in the United States. However, gender ideology also provides an essential part of the answer. A male-breadwinner model in Canada was enforced through moral ideology that held that the role of women was in the home and concrete policy decisions that made it harder for women to work. In Canada's early history, these policy decisions were made at the provincial level, while during World War II the same breadwinner model was reinforced by national policy. The prevailing discourse in Canada for many years was one where working mothers were socially condemned and the nuclear household with a working father and unpaid mother who provided all the childcare was the ideal. Much as in several European countries, this gender ideology conflicted with demand for school lunches and made it impossible for children's advocates to ask for them. Further, the policy response to this ideology ignored the issue of child malnutrition, obscuring another issue around which demand for school lunches could organize.

The ideal of the nuclear household was entrenched early in Canadian ideology. In the early 1900s, only those single mothers who were deemed respectable by the standards of social workers and volunteers were able to receive state aid. The standards of respectability depended on middle-class ideas of womanhood and focused on celibacy and house cleanliness (Finkel 2006, 102). At this point in time, a pattern of state morality that reflected certain views about the family began to be codified, as women who never married or who voluntarily left their husbands were denied any assistance in all the provinces. Throughout the first half of the twentieth century, these ideals of motherhood and womanhood were reinforced by a society that saw motherhood as a full-time job and condemned women who attempted to work outside the home. Demands for mother's allowances increased across Canada following World War I due to the number of widowed mothers or women with injured husbands. Support for mother's allowances differed by province, but most provinces provided some aid by the 1930s (Finkel 2006, 101). No province provided aid to single mothers, continuing the state's moral condemnation of single mothers. In addition, mother's allowances worked to keep women out of the workforce and dependent on the state in the same way that otherwise married women were kept dependent on their husbands.

One of the first national social policy programs put into place by the Canadian government, following aid for veterans, was a family allowance. Much as in other states, the family allowance system was gendered, acting to keep married women out of the workforce. Family allowances were created as a political compromise by the Mackenzie King government. While King rejected the majority of the Marsh Report's proposals,[4] his government was aware of the public's demand for government reform. Looking for some social program to create in order to appease public demand, King chose family allowances as they were in the Marsh Report and supported by the report's Subcommittee on the Status of Women. The hope was to buy the government time to consider further social reforms. Under the Family Allowance Act of 1944, benefits were payable to all children, through their mothers, at a monthly rate to help maintain the child. This was commonly referred to as the "baby bonus" as it was a universal program not based on need or income. In the late 1940s, working-class and rural families were able to gain 10 to 30 percent of their income from the family allowances, although those percentages eroded over time as the program did not keep pace with inflation. As a political move, the allowance system was designed to weaken union support by evening out the wages between married and unmarried workers (Finkel 2006, 131). They were also designed to encourage married women, who had been called into the workforce during World War II, to go back to the home, as the government thought it unlikely that the economy would recover enough to provide full employment if women were included in the workforce. The allowances were to partially compensate women for the wages they would forgo by leaving work. In addition, the government hoped to create a monopoly for men over the better-paying jobs in the labor market.

In addition to the family allowances, married women were forced back into the home by the removal of federal subsidies for day care, guarantees that veterans would get their jobs back, and reduction of the income tax deduction for married women's work. Further, the federal government put a restriction on the hiring of married women that lasted until 1955. Of this, one of the most problematic for mothers was the lack of childcare. The choices for some women, particularly poor or single mothers, were stark: either drop out of the workforce and attempt to subsist on the family allowance or find whatever childcare they could. There was pervasive government propaganda supporting the ideal of a nuclear family with a stay-at-home mother and a working father. This was so pervasive "as to virtually make invisible the many women who both raised children and worked outside the home" (Finkel 2006, 194). The government worked to reinforce these values through advertising schemes that made it clear that a married woman's accepted role was in the home.

TABLE 4.1 Percentage of Married Women in the Workforce

Year	Canada	United States	United Kingdom
1930	n/a	11.7	10.6
1940	4.1	13.8	n/a
1950	10	21.6	32.6
1960	22.9	30.6	32.5

SOURCES: Canada statistics are from Finkel 2006, 198; the U.S. and U.K. statistics are from Costa 2000, 106.

The Canadian government's efforts were successful. Compared to both the United Kingdom and the United States, a far smaller number of married women were in the workforce from 1930 to 1960. Table 4.1 shows there are many more married, working women in the United States and United Kingdom than in Canada, particularly after World War II. This is due to federal, provincial, and employer policies that were biased against married women. The Canadian state used policy and advertising to get married women back into the home, reflecting economic concerns that there were not enough jobs in the economy for every person and a gendered idea of how households should work.

The family allowances, other policies encouraging women to return to the home, and pervasive propaganda about the nuclear family help explain why Canada does not have a school lunch program. First, because mothers were expected to stay home and care for the children, there were not the same concerns that occurred in other countries when mothers were at work and could not be expected to feed the children during the day. Second, the family allowances were to be used by the family for the care of the child—absolving the government of other care. Third, and relatedly, the family allowances worked, at least initially, to gloss over the problem of child poverty. How could there be child poverty when every child was provided a monthly allowance from the federal government? While poverty was discussed and targeted at the national level, most prominently in the "war on poverty round" that began in 1965 with a new federal pension plan and a federal/provincial grant program (Ismael 2006, 28), child poverty did not appear as a particular issue until 1989. This is different from the United States and United Kingdom where targeted concerns with child poverty began in the late 1800s. Because child poverty was not seen as a particularly important issue, it was impossible for voluntary organizations to mobilize around the issue and create culturally resonant frames that would highlight the issue of child malnutrition. In addition, unlike in the United States, the war did not bring the issue of child malnutrition to the fore, closing off that avenue of action.

THE UNITED STATES VERSUS CANADA

Comparing the contexts of the United States and Canada, where material conditions were similar, demonstrates the necessity of including ideational factors in analysis of this social policy. Both countries had similar agricultural policies and similar problems of agricultural surplus, but in the United States these surpluses were channeled toward feeding children, while in Canada these surpluses were either donated abroad, sold for export, or accumulated in government warehouses. In addition, both countries had broadly similar gender ideologies; while Canada's efforts to keep married women out of the workplace were somewhat more draconian than the policies of the United States, no one could claim that the United States was anything but a male-breadwinner society at the time. In the United States, the Lanham Act had created childcare centers to enable women to work during the war; these were rapidly shut down once the war was over in an effort to force women out of the labor market (Cohen 1996). Thus both countries were broadly similar across both agricultural policy and gender ideology.

Their differing trajectories in regards to school lunches can be explained by the focus, in the United States, on child poverty, the connection created between agriculture and schools during the Great Depression, and the ability of actors in the United States to successfully connect these two issues under the banner of national security. In Canada, farmers and consumers never forced the government to use agricultural goods domestically, and thus there were no extant programs upon which to build. In addition, demands for social policy reform were met by the creation of family allowances, thus silencing critics of Canada's antipoverty and gender policy. One of the major differences between the countries was the issue of child poverty, which in the United States was highlighted during the war, when a surprising number of men were rejected by the army due to malnutrition. In Canada this did not happen, and the issue of child poverty remained undiscussed long after the war, hidden by a gender ideology that kept women at home and responsible for the health and welfare of their children.

In the United States, a concern with future security and the necessity of well-fed children for that security goal provided an opportunity for proponents of feeding children to argue for the creation of the national school lunch program. In Canada, these concerns did not trump attitudes about gender, which shut down the possibility of a program before it could even be imagined. Ideas proved integral to both the creation and non-creation of a program in these two similar countries, much as they did throughout Europe. Just as in Europe, each country, with its specific politics, prioritized different ideas. While in both countries there was a desire to remove women from the workforce and a gender ideology that saw women's role as firmly in the home, in the United States a concern with security fostered the creation of a program that could, in fact, be considered women-friendly. However, the U.S. program would not have been possible without the connection forged between agricultural interests and schools ten years prior. These material concerns became even more important during the next phase of school lunch program emergence, as the agricultural interests of the United States propelled the creation of the Word Food Programme, but ideas still played a role in justifying the creation of both the WFP and school meals as a central pillar of their agenda. However, the ideas that matter shifted dramatically to those that concern children and economic development rather than security, women, or welfare.

5 · THE SECOND WAVE

The U.N.'s World Food Programme

The World Food Programme, or WFP, was involved in school lunches from its inception. Why it did so provides further evidence for my argument that ideational contexts combined with material agricultural surpluses, in this case the surpluses created by the United States, to produce school lunch programs. By the time the WFP was created, a concern with women and the ways in which school lunch programs could benefit them had disappeared from the conversation, and instead attention was focused on children. This shift reflected the thinking of George McGovern, the primary architect of the WFP, and the emergence of development as an overriding ideational framework in the international community.

The WFP is the organization in the U.N. system that is exclusively concerned with food aid, and it is the primary conduit of food aid for development and emergency relief in the world. Its sister organization is the Food and Agriculture Organization (FAO), which is concerned with food production. The mandate of the WFP is to use food aid to support economic and social development, provide food and associated logistics support in times of emergency, and generally promote world food security (WFP 2014a). According to the WFP website, the aims of the WFP are to "save lives, improve nutrition and quality of life of the world's most vulnerable people at critical times in their lives, [and to] enable development by helping people build assets that benefit them directly and promoting the self-reliance of poor people and communities." The logic behind the WFP's development projects is that food aid will temporarily free "the poor of the need to provide food for their families, which gives them the time and resources to invest in lasting assets such as better houses, clinics and schools, new agricultural skills and technology." An early development project focused on providing food to migrants in order to give them the time to settle and cultivate their land (Hall 2007); a current project in Ethiopia provides food to workers who are building earthworks to prevent water runoff (WFP 2013).

School feeding programs have been an important component of WFP aid since its inception in 1961. In the initial U.N. Food and Agriculture Organization study, which laid out the foundations of the WFP, it was suggested that resources be made available for social development. School feeding programs, as an integral part of human capital formation, were recommended for support at the rate of $500 million a year (Shaw 2001, 24). In 2013, the WFP provided meals to 20 million children in sixty-three countries (WFP 2014b).[1] Figure 5.1 shows the historical growth of WFP programs. The majority of programs were started in either the 1960s, immediately after the creation of the WFP, or the 1970s. Almost all of the programs were extended, expanded, or had their budgets increased in subsequent years. In other words, once the WFP became involved in a country, it typically stayed involved in that country until the program was phased out, in the 1990s or

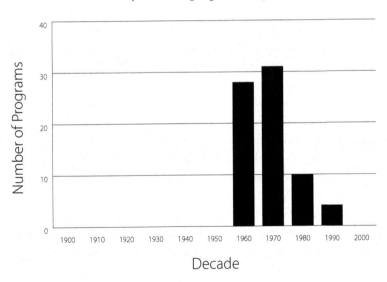

FIGURE 5.1. New WFP-Sponsored Programs, by Decade
Sources: See the appendix.

2000s.[2] Many of the African programs that still exist today were started in either the 1960s or 1970s. To a certain extent, then, this is why so few programs were created in the 1990s–2000s—those countries that needed the programs had had them created in the early years of the WFP.[3]

The objectives in WFP school feeding programs are to improve nutrition and health, increase school attendance by children of poor households (particularly girls), and encourage more regular school attendance. These objectives are related to improved human capital and a country's long-term development prospects, goals to which the WFP has been devoted since its inception. Development emerged as an important part of the international discourse in the late 1950s and early 1960s as newly decolonized countries brought these concerns to the forefront. Thus, the idea of development was uniquely available and positioned for use by policy entrepreneurs in the early 1960s, and was the central idea that determined the direction of WFP policy at that time.

The concept of development used in the early 1960s was contested, and policy prescriptions for the issue were evolving as well. Beginning in the 1950s and 1960s, as former colonies became independent, scholars and policy makers began to study and debate the reasons for these countries' so-called backwardness. The field of development has always been contested, with some focusing on political development, by which they mean the creation of liberal democracies, others focusing on social development, and still others focusing on economic development and the construction of capitalist economies (Kohli 2004). The very terms *developing, underdeveloped*, and *development* are contested, as they can suggest value judgments (Handelman 2009). Those who thought the primary reason for underdevelopment was due to culture debated those who blamed the legacy of colonialism for the lack of political, economic, and social growth. These debates revolved around the role of the state and whether or not development was best accomplished through statist or free-trade models (Kanbur 2004). They spilled into the United Nations, putting the contested idea of development on the agenda and making it available as a frame for actors concerned with agricultural surpluses, and giving those concerned with child malnutrition a newly resonant language with which to make their case. While the scholarly debates continued, the newly enlarged presence of developing countries in the United Nations helped focus the U.N. agenda on efforts to eliminate not only poverty but also hunger, illiteracy, and disease (Jackson 2008). These concerns were emphasized by the United Nations during the first Decade of Development, which started in January 1961, and focused on a more holistic understanding of development.

While development by the 1980s became synonymous with International Monetary Fund (IMF) calls to reduce state involvement in the economy, in the 1960s the developmental thought that won out called explicitly for state involvement in the economy (Rapley 2007, 2). In particular, state involvement focused on the development of industry and the creation of infrastructure and human capital to support industry. During the Decade of Development, the United Nations focused on "growth plus change" and worked to help developing countries achieve economic growth as well as social development (Jolly 2010). This focus on economic and social development became very important as the WFP was founded, and in particular the idea of human capital, which encompassed both economic and social development, would prove foundational in the WFP's understanding of its mission and the projects it chose to fund.

The promotion of human capital as an integral component of development emerged in 1960 with work by Theodore Schultz, and the 1960s were devoted to work on the topic (Blaug 1976, 827). While there are any number of variations on human capital theory, the core, based in liberal economic theory, holds that people invest in themselves with an eye to the future. This contention was easily expanded to the level of the state, with a number of studies that connected state investment in education to national productivity gains (Becker 2009). The development of human capital theory and its rapid growth as a field of study was a cognitive paradigm that provided a direction for policy makers as they puzzled over the problems of hunger and illiteracy. There was new evidence that connected a cause (education) with an effect (national productivity). As such, it provided a new way for policy makers to understand their choices, particularly those involving children and education. This new ideational factor, when considered in conjunction with the agricultural interests of the United States, explains the adoption of the school lunch programs by the WFP. It provided a framework for U.S. policy makers like George McGovern to justify the creation of WFP school lunch programs while they were predominately driven by U.S. agricultural policy goals.

U.S. FOOD AID

The United States was the primary architect of and, initially, chief donor to the WFP. As such, it is imperative to understand the history of U.S. food aid in order to understand the creation of the WFP and its inclusion of school lunch programs, as the WFP would not have existed were it not for the institutional structures created by the U.S. food aid program. The first international, long-term food aid provided by the U.S. Congress followed the end of World War I. Relief was primarily supplied to "the various dismembered parts of the Austro-Hungarian Empire and of Germany," as well as Finland, the Balkan States, and parts of Belgium and France (Singer, Wood, and Jennings 1987, 18). Some 6.23 million tons of food were shipped between 1918 and 1926. Not only did this food provide nourishment as these countries began their war recovery efforts, but it provided an outlet for American food surpluses that had built up due to wartime agricultural requirements. This combination of idealism and pragmatism set the stage for future food aid programs, and particularly the WFP, and reflects my basic contention that examining both ideational and material factors is necessary for understanding policy emergence.

The next big international food aid program was the Marshall Plan, in which $3.5 billion of food, feed, and fertilizer was transferred primarily from the United States and Canada to Europe. The food aspects of the Marshall Plan proceeded extremely smoothly, due to the previous experience of supplying food after World War I as well as the creation during the 1930s of the U.S. Commodity Credit Corporation (CCC). This organization was created by executive order on October 16, 1933, for the purpose of buying and selling agricultural commodities and making loans to farmers in order to maintain price supports and production controls. The CCC was the vehicle for managing agricultural surpluses and providing farmer subsidies. The CCC emerged directly from the Great Depression and U.S. government concerns with falling farm income. Due to its experience in managing surpluses, the United States was easily able to implement the Marshall Plan.[4]

Once Europe began to recover, demand for U.S. farm products began to decline. Not only was Europe beginning to become food self-sufficient again, but there was not a large market for U.S. imports elsewhere. However, during both World War I and World War II American farmers had been encouraged to increase production significantly in order to supply not only U.S. troops but U.S. allies. In addition, price supports had been solidified during World War II, in part to deal with the surpluses that had been encouraged by an aggressive price support policy during the Great Depression (Winders 2009). These price supports, the core of the agricultural welfare state, encouraged production, which led to agricultural surpluses, especially of those foods that were heavily subsidized (Sheingate 2003). For instance, after a banner year in 1953, wheat reserves rose from 13 million tons to over 42 million tons. The surplus held by the U.S. government was 25 million tons, equal to the level of world trade in wheat (Singer, Wood, and Jennings 1987, 22).

These surpluses were a danger to U.S. agricultural prices and producer incomes. The Korean War had just ended, reducing the immediate need of agricultural surpluses by the army as well as cementing the Cold War into place. The agricultural lobbies, and particularly the grain traders, drove the passage of PL 480, which became the core of U.S. food aid policy. Under the Marshall Plan, grain companies such as Cargill and Archer Daniel Midlands acted as government agents in disbursing grain, using the network of trading contacts they had established in the 1930s when they expanded their businesses internationally (Broehl 1992; Kneen 2002). These companies were well positioned to lobby for an agricultural act that would act as "a market expansion programme wrapped in the American flag of anti-communism" (Kneen 2002, 142) and they got what they wanted. Using food aid to sway countries away from Soviet influence was always one of the underlying objectives of the U.S. food aid program (Mousseau 2005). It was the twin concerns of agricultural surpluses and the containment of communism that led to PL 480, again demonstrating the interaction between ideational and material factors. Grain traders used ideas about communism in order to accomplish their material goals.

PL 480, the Agricultural Trade Development and Assistance Act, was enacted by the Eighty-third Congress and signed by President Dwight Eisenhower on July 10, 1954. PL 480 used a variety of methods to provide food aid including "commodity sales to be paid for in the currency of the recipient country" (Leach 1994, 3),[5] donations to voluntary organizations such as CARE or Catholic Relief Services of surplus commodities for use both in the United States and abroad, and government-to-government food donations for famine relief. In the very first year of operation,

3.4 million metric tons of food were distributed; this rose to 14 million metric tons of food two years later (Leach 1994, 3). There were a great many agricultural products driving U.S. domestic and international policy decisions.

Despite its supposed foreign policy and humanitarian objectives, this act was clearly focused on national economic goals. Eisenhower declared that it would "lay the basis for a permanent expansion of our exports of agricultural products with lasting benefits to ourselves and peoples of other lands."[6] In the first decade of the program, the emphasis was almost entirely on disposing of the American agricultural surplus. This emphasis completely overshadowed the humanitarian objectives. Unfortunately, the American surplus was so great and the price support system encouraged production at such a high level, that a domestic surplus continued to build. There were other problems with the program. For instance, some countries began to accumulate large U.S.-owned soft currency reserves (Leach 1994, 4). This raised concerns about the potential for destabilization in developing countries due to the amount of control the United States had over the money supply (Ruttan 1993, 8). And in spite of the exports, new markets for American agricultural products failed to appear, to the frustration of the program's architects.

Due to inefficiencies and frustrations with the program, some changes began to be made as early as 1959.[7] In 1959, Senate Bill 1711 changed the name of PL 480 to the International Food for Peace Act. This new title primarily reflects the work of Senators Hubert Humphrey and James Fulbright, who envisioned U.S. agricultural supplies working effectively to "build the world conditions for peace" (U.S. Senate Foreign Relations Committee 1959) and to reduce human hunger. Humphrey was acutely aware of the potential for food to work as a weapon in the Cold War to win countries over to the American side (Clapp 2012; Lappe, Collins, and Fowler 1977). The new name reflected an international conversation that had begun to occur about the connections between hunger, peace, and development. Thus there was some shift in United States thinking in the late 1950s that the use of agricultural surpluses for peace and hunger relief was more important than simply aiding the American economy. The importance of the idea of international development was beginning to make inroads into U.S. policy making.

John F. Kennedy's election also presaged a new era in how the United States used food aid. Agricultural issues initially bored Kennedy, but Senator Humphrey and Representative George McGovern pushed the idea of food for peace on him in such a way, linking agriculture with foreign policy, that he soon became a strong proponent of the idea (McGovern 2001, 50). Kennedy began to work closely with Rep. McGovern in honing his ideas on food for peace. McGovern was crucial for the further development of U.S. food aid.

George McGovern was born and raised in South Dakota, eventually serving as both representative and senator from that state. McGovern was not raised as a farmer (his father was a pastor), but growing up on the plains of South Dakota in the 1920s–1930s, he saw clearly the importance, and the plight, of farmers. His government career was marked by a commitment to farmers, food security, and a multilateral approach to the solution of world problems (Shaw 2001, 8). During an interview in 2004 with the *Minneapolis Star Tribune*, McGovern spoke about the first time he witnessed hunger and the long-lasting effects of that experience:

> I've been interested in hunger since the Second World War, when I arrived in Naples harbor as a bomber pilot. There were several hundred hungry kids lined up on the docks on either side of our ship, shouting to us: "Babe Ruth! Butterfinger!" And the captain's voice came over the loudspeaker, telling us not to throw anything to them. An American troop ship had come in yesterday and they started throwing candy bars, and some of it fell in the water and a couple of dozen kids drowned scrambling for that food. I'd never seen hungry people before. I grew up in South Dakota, in the Depression. We were poor, everybody was poor, but very few didn't have enough to eat.

McGovern was inspired to work on issues of hunger and to consider the link between hunger and children.

Throughout his career, McGovern advocated for the reduction of world hunger. McGovern's consideration of school lunches as an important type of food aid is well documented, as was his contention that children were one of the most important recipients of food aid. He was always particularly concerned with feeding hungry children and long pushed for international school lunch programs, first through the WFP and then by lobbying the U.S. government to create the McGovern-Dole International Food for Education and Child Nutrition Program, which was created in 2002. In his letter of resignation from the Food for Peace office in 1963, which he left to seek a Senate office, he spoke generally of the achievement of food aid and then gave one priority recommendation, urging "that the United States take an even more active lead in providing a daily school lunch for every needy child in the world. No form of overseas assistance could return greater dividends for so little cost. We should undertake this task with renewed energy 'because it is right'" (Shaw 2001, 16). McGovern believed that school meals were one of the best tools to aid development in the third world because he saw educating children as key to improving a country's human capital (McGovern 2001, 31).

At McGovern's urging, Kennedy gave a historic speech at the Mitchell, South Dakota, Corn Palace that summed up his thinking on the issues: "I don't regard the agricultural surplus as a problem. I regard it as an opportunity to use the food imaginatively, not only for our own people, but for people all around the world. . . . we recognize that food is strength, and food is peace, and food is freedom, and food is a helping hand to people around the world whose good will and friendship we want" (McGovern 2001, 50).

In the first days of Kennedy's term, in his second Executive Order, Kennedy brought the Food for Peace program directly into the White House and appointed George McGovern to be director. By bringing the office into the White House, Kennedy removed the program from bureaucratic impediments that would likely have cropped up had the office been located in either the State Department or the Department of Agriculture. One of McGovern's first moves was to use the power of language to cement the idea that this new food for peace program was about peace by directing his staff to stop talking about "surplus disposal": "We were in the business of feeding children, not disposing of garbage. Anyone who wanted to be in the disposal business should apply to the D.C. sanitation department" (McGovern 2001, 52). He was well aware of the way in which ideas could influence action. McGovern played a powerful role as director of Food for Peace. He expanded the role of PL 480 toward more humanitarian and development objectives with the introduction of a number of Food for Wages projects, and by 1963, 1 million tons of food were being shipped under Food for Peace auspices. In addition, he was the primary architect of the World Food Programme (Shaw 2001, 6).

PRECURSORS TO THE WORLD FOOD PROGRAMME

While the United States was moving forward on its own food aid programs, the international community as a whole was also moving toward
more constructive uses of food aid. There were two attempts to form an
international food aid organization before the WFP was formed. The first
was a proposal from the director-general of the FAO, Sir John Boyd Orr, in
1946. Boyd Orr recommended a series of actions to deal with the world's
food problems. He proposed, in a general way, a World Food Board that
would work to increase "the productive power of the great masses of people in the underdeveloped worlds" as well as "enable farmers in the highly
developed areas to go ahead producing for the world's needs without the
fear and the fact of surpluses and ruinous prices" (FAO 1946, 12). Boyd
Orr argued that this could best be accomplished under the auspices of
the U.N., and he suggested that loans to increase production, technical
assistance for farming projects, and an international food storage system
were the essential elements of a World Food Board. However, his attempt
to "reconcile the interests of producers and consumers of agriculture and
trade" was not approved, largely due to the "power of sovereignty and
self-interest" (Singer, Wood, and Jennings 1987, 27); countries wanted to
maintain control over their agricultural products and pricing. Further, the
Soviet Union was not in favor of this proposal, as it was "cynically suspi-
cious" that such an organization would primarily be used to promote U.S.
foreign policy interests (Shaw 2007, 27).

In 1955 M. Ezekiel's study "Uses of Agricultural Surpluses to finance
Economic Development in Under-Developed Countries" was published by the FAO and it explored, using India as a case study, the way
food could help promote economic development. It was the first study to
systematically link food aid and economic development and, strikingly,
shifted the focus from reducing surpluses in developed countries to using
surpluses to aid other countries. This study inspired the second attempt
to create an international food aid organization, which was proposed in
1956 by Senator Humphrey in the United States. Humphrey, concerned
with the problem of world hunger and the relationship between hunger,
peace, and development, brought two resolutions to the Senate Committee on Foreign Relations suggesting the creation of a World Food Bank
and/or an International Food and Raw Materials Reserve. These were

debated in a subcommittee of the Committee on Foreign Relations and Senator Humphrey took a leading role in discussing these resolutions.[8] The first resolution, Senate Resolution 85, urged the president to consult with the United Nations to make a food bank, modeled after the International Bank for Reconstruction and Development, from which member nations could borrow food or fibers.[9] The second resolution, Senate Resolution 86, asked the president to consult with the United Nations in order to establish a reserve to store excess farm products and other raw materials in order to avoid price fluctuations. Both of these resolutions were designed, in Senator Humphrey's words, "To convert the burden of temporary excess production in single countries into a blessing for all nations. Both are designed to convert temporary surpluses from being a disturbing factor in domestic markets and in international economic relations, into what they can and should be—a powerful force for human well-being and peace among nations of the world" (U.S. Senate 1956, 3). This statement explicitly connects the productive use of food surpluses with development.

Senator Humphrey was convinced that PL 480 was not sufficient to handle the growing problem of hunger in the world. He wanted a U.N.-organized agency that would deal with hunger due to his belief in multilateral solutions to world problems. He was aware that the United States was being accused of "dumping" its agricultural surpluses on the world market, and he saw the advantages of a multilateral agency to defuse these concerns (U.S. Senate 1956, 90). Further, he was interested in using food as a tool in the Cold War, in order to reward U.S. allies or sway other countries toward U.S. interests. Resolutions are designed to express the opinion of a committee or a congressional body, and no action is required from a resolution. Neither of these resolutions made it out of the subcommittee. However, the mere discussion of these resolutions laid the ground for congressional acceptance of the World Food Programme.

A further step was taken by the United States toward the WFP in 1960, before Kennedy was elected president. On August 24, 1959, the Committee on Foreign Relations passed the International Food for Peace Resolution. This resolution expressed the support of Congress for the president to explore an international food program and saw the purposes of that program as "combating extreme price fluctuations in the international market in food products, alleviating famine and starvation, helping absorb temporary market surpluses of farm products and economic and social development programs" (U.S. Senate 1959). This resolution gave the president permission, and urged him, to endorse a multilateral food program at the U.N. General Assembly meeting in September 1960. A letter accompanied this report from the acting secretary of state, C. Douglas Dillon, that indicated the president's desire to have the United Nations develop a plan for feeding hungry people. The president's letter points out that it is "an objective of the United States to increase the prestige, authority, and effectiveness of the United Nations system," as well as the fact that "there are some developed areas where the recipient countries definitely prefer to receive foreign assistance through the United Nations system" (U.S. Senate 1959). This letter is a clear acknowledgment of the political expediency of multilateral, rather than bilateral, food aid, and demonstrates the necessity of material factors in the creation of policy.

CREATION OF THE WFP

When George McGovern was appointed to lead the U.S. Food for Peace program, several key things were in place to make the creation of the WFP more likely. The first was that Kennedy was devoted to participating in the United Nations in a more serious manner than some of his predecessors. Related, there was a greater commitment within the U.N. to multilateral activity than there had been previously. The second was that, as we have seen, a number of international food programs had been proposed both internationally and at the domestic, U.S. level. Thus, the idea of a multilateral food program was not new and the reasons for it had been laid out in several earlier documents, such as Boyd Orr's proposal and Senate Resolutions 85 and 86. The third was the positioning of George McGovern in the U.S. government and B. R. Sen at the FAO, two men who had a strong vision for and commitment to using agricultural surpluses for humanitarian objectives (Shaw 2001, 8). The fourth was the emergence of development as a policy priority in the late 1950s–early 1960s as developing countries put their concerns on the international agenda. Development concerns had emerged as one of the top issues of the 1960s, and the United Nations declared the 1960s the Decade of Development. Fifth, and relatedly, the explicit connection between education and national productivity had been developed as human capital theory in the early 1960s and provided a new cognitive paradigm for policy makers as they puzzled out how to promote development and use agricultural surpluses.

The seeds of the WFP can be traced to the Freedom from Hunger Campaign. This campaign was an FAO project started by Sen in 1960 and was planned to coincide with the U.N.'s Decade of Development. Sen was an Indian diplomat and had studied food and malnutrition issues since his experience as a relief commissioner during the Bengal famine of 1942–43. He speaks in his autobiography of the "profound and abiding sense of guilt" suffered by all who were involved in the famine (B. Sen 1982, 50). This experience led him to focus on hunger issues and the role that food aid could play in alleviating hunger. In particular, he speaks of his lifelong dream of a world without degrading poverty and hunger. Sen was acutely aware of the cognitive paradigm connecting development and food aid. He carried these convictions into his diplomatic postings and particularly his tenure as the FAO's director-general from 1956 to 1967. Based on these convictions, he worked to transform the FAO from a technical organization into a development agency (B. Sen 1982, 123).

Sen's Freedom from Hunger campaign was primarily an educational campaign to bring attention in the international community to issues of malnutrition and hunger. As conceived by Sen, the campaign was devoted to bringing attention to the issues of hunger, securing the participation of all concerned parties, raising the enthusiasm of those parties, and establishing a higher level of "mutually profitable world trade to help raise the prosperity of both developed and developing countries" (B. Sen 1982, 138). In light of this campaign and the new emphasis on development, the U.N. General Assembly passed a resolution in 1960 on the Provision of Food Surpluses to Food-Deficient Peoples through the U.N. system.[10] This resolution, after endorsing the Freedom from Hunger Campaign and recognizing the need for economic development in underdeveloped countries, called for the Food and Agriculture Organization of the United Nations to create procedures for disposing of surplus agricultural goods (U.N. 1960). In response to the General Assembly Resolution, a small group of experts was convened by Sen to consider what sort of procedures might work for the disposal of food surpluses (Luhe 1986, 2:11).

Under Sen's direction, the expert group produced a study titled *Development Through Food: A Strategy for Surplus Utilization*. The study was "the first authoritative and responsible position treating food surpluses positively as potential contributions to economic development and growth, rather than negatively as an unwanted load to be got rid of with the least harmful effects" (Luhe 1986, 2:15). Its focus was clearly influenced by the development discourse prevalent in the U.N. system at that time. The study called for food surpluses to be used for economic and social development, for countries to make their own decisions regarding food aid (rather than donor countries making the decisions), for developing projects only within the overall context of a country's development program, and, finally, that the use of food surpluses should not endanger the local economy (Sen 1982, 200). This last principle was to guide the creation of the WFP and influence the inclusion of school lunch programs, as the architects insisted that the use of food aid must not interfere with domestic markets in the recipient country and that food aid ought to increase consumption, rather than divert consumption.

The report also focused on the formation of human capital and stressed that it was "as basic, as necessary and as productive as physical capital formation" (Luhe, 1986, 2: chapter 12, 1). This focus on human capital built on human capital theory and became central to the discussions that would result in the WFP. The study drew fine distinctions between economic programs, social programs, and land reform programs. Some of these categories would be condensed within the WFP. Despite these general admonitions, the study contained no specific proposals for action. However, it did convey the idea that the FAO was ready and willing to play its part in the organization of information and coordination and distribution of food aid, dependent on what member countries envisioned as its role (FAO 1961b).

An FAO Intergovernmental Advisory Committee was held April 5–12, 1961, in order to discuss its study. This meeting was largely concerned with the minutia of the study and included extensive conversation on the issue of how a multilateral program might coordinate bilateral food transfers. The group also discussed how the FAO might begin to take on the responsibility of promoting economic development, which historically was considered to lay with the United Nations. On the third day of the meeting, April 7, an ad hoc group was convened to prepare the report for the larger meeting. This ad hoc group included representatives from the United States, Netherlands, Canada, France, Ghana, and Pakistan as well as Sen.

McGovern had been asked by Kennedy to represent the United States at this meeting (Shaw 2001, 6) and was part of the U.S. delegation at the ad hoc group. The first day of the ad hoc meeting included conversations about the specific wording of phrases in the report, whether multilateral arrangements were useful to pursue, how much authority the FAO ought to be granted if a multilateral arrangement was approved, and whether emergency food needs were more important to pursue than social or development food aid (FAO 1961a). This issue was particularly contentious, with some country delegations like Canada and the Netherlands advocating that the FAO only take on emergency feeding situations, and other countries, such as Pakistan, India, and France, stressing the need for economic or social programs for development. In fact, Pakistan specifically wanted to avoid any FAO role in emergency feeding out of a concern that this would expand the FAO's role past its constitutional abilities.

The only contribution McGovern offered during that first meeting was agreement with the Canadian delegation that a multilateral arrangement for food surpluses would be desirable and that "the United States delegation felt that some part of the initial effort should be devoted to school lunch programs and labor-intensive projects, as a means of giving FAO some operational experience" (FAO 1961a). This was the only mention of school lunches at the meeting. Given McGovern's commitment to school lunches and his understanding of their importance as a development tool, it is unsurprising that he brought it up. The other substantive position taken by the U.S. delegation was a statement that the group work to "develop recommendations . . . to the Director-General for concrete proposals that would result in action" (FAO 1961a). The U.S. delegation, more than others, was thinking in terms of concrete plans of action.

Over that weekend, McGovern asked his staff to come up with a proposal that would make concrete the FAO's study about the benefits of food aid and received permission from Kennedy to propose a program with a "fund of $100 million in commodities and cash contributions. For its part, the United States would be prepared to offer $40 million in commodities, and the possibility of a supplementary cash contribution will be explored in Washington" (McGovern 1964, 108). McGovern submitted his proposal during the meeting of the ad hoc group on Monday morning. The chairman of the meeting asked McGovern if the United States was changing its position on the study, which it had already submitted. McGovern replied that he was suggesting some specific action to implement the broad objectives outlined in the report (FAO 1961a). This was a surprise to the other members of the delegation who had not planned to do anything but give advice to the FAO (Shaw 2001, 7).

The proposal, in addition to the promised money, suggested an experimental period for the World Food Programme of three years and committed the program to work primarily on emergencies, school lunch programs, and other labor-intensive projects in order to develop experience for the organization in managing different kinds of projects. It was an exceedingly detailed proposal, reflecting McGovern's ideological commitments and political pragmatism by speaking directly to U.S. concerns about its own program, PL 480 (Shaw 2001, 8). The WFP would be restricted to project aid, not the kind of large-scale, bulk program food aid that the United States and others provided bilaterally. The United States wanted no reduction in its ability to sell its commodities through Title I activities. In addition, in order to prove that the WFP was complementary to, rather than competing with, PL 480, its focus was to be on social projects rather than economic or market development, thus, the emphasis on projects such as school lunches or food-for-work programs.

The delegates from other countries were surprised by the proposal, and even recessed to discuss whether or not it was serious, but quickly accepted it. The immediate reaction at the meeting was one of profound gratitude both for the amount of the U.S. contribution and the clear U.S. commitment to multilateral food aid efforts. In particular, Canada, Ghana, the Netherlands, and France spoke in support of the proposal (FAO 1961a).

Kennedy endorsed it in a press conference on April 21, 1961, making it clear that the United States was committed to the new program. Both McGovern and Sen worked within their communities over the next six months to ensure its passage. Because of the large commitment of the United States and Kennedy's desire to use food surpluses in a multilateral way, U.S. acceptance of the plan was key. McGovern had to reconcile the interests of the U.S. delegates to the United Nations, who wanted a much larger food aid organization that would focus on economic and social development, with the interests of the U.S. State Department, which wanted a smaller, experimental program that would focus on emergencies (Shaw 2001, 10). The WFP proposal, which provided a role for emergencies and school feeding but not necessarily other social and economic programs, was a compromise between these two competing U.S. interests. School lunch programs were more acceptable to those people that wanted only emergency aid because feeding children is more politically palatable than other kinds of projects and fit well with the dominant cognitive paradigm of human capital theory. In addition, school lunch programs provide immediate nutritional relief and can be partially regarded as emergency feeding. McGovern was aware of these considerations and understandings about school lunch programs when he made his proposal, and it was his pragmatic consideration of these competing positions that led him to insert school lunches into the original formulation and helped create U.S. acceptance of the program before the U.N. General Assembly meeting.

Sen worked to ensure the passage of the World Food Programme first by the FAO and then by the General Assembly. Like McGovern, Sen had to find compromise positions between the countries (mostly developing countries) that were more interested in social and economic food aid and those more interested in providing only emergency food aid (mostly developed countries; B. Sen 1982, 196). In addition, Sen had to work with McGovern to make sure that any compromise in the FAO would be greeted favorably by the United States, the largest party that had committed financially to the new organization. Sen was able to accomplish this compromise in the same way as McGovern, by insisting that emergency aid receive top billing but that school lunches be included as a specific social and economic program. Countries that refused to accept other social and economic development programs found school lunch programs more acceptable, probably because children are regarded as more vulnerable than adults and more in need of protection, and due to the cognitive paradigm of human capital theory, which was a top concern in the international system at the time. Sen was responsible for moving the original proposal through the FAO as a whole and then into the General Assembly. He worked to keep school lunches in the final document in order to provide a compromise position between countries that wanted more aid for social and economic programs and countries that wanted aid only for emergency purposes.

By November, the FAO had created the "FAO/U.N. Proposal Regarding Procedures and Arrangements for Multilateral Utilization of Surplus Foods." This proposal was much more specific than McGovern's original proposal and included the specific rules of the WFP, which as the time was called SUD, Surplus Utilization Division. This proposal was composed of "arrangements to be made by countries in providing the resources needed, and by FAO and other cooperating international organizations in creating the mechanisms for handling these resources; and then secondly in terms of the procedures to be followed by recipient countries, contributing countries, and international organizations respectively" (FAO 1961c).

The proposal contained all the elements in McGovern's original proposal, including the beginning fund of $100 million and the focus on emergency food aid, school lunch projects, and labor-intensive projects (FAO 1961c). Because the organization that was created dovetailed so closely with McGovern's original proposal, McGovern is credited with "getting the World Food Programme off the ground" (Luhe 1986, 1:17). Likewise, the only official history of the World Food Programme considers the WFP to be one of the few international organizations created in such a personal way, based on one man's initiative and inspiration (Shaw 2001).[11]

On November 24, 1961, the FAO passed resolution No 1/61, "Utilization of Food Surpluses—World Food Programme," and on December 19, 1961, the General Assembly passed Resolution 1714. This resolution authorized the creation of the WFP as a three-year experimental program with $100 million in contributions to be administered jointly under the authority of the FAO and the United Nations. This new program was to focus on food emergencies, school feeding, and implementing pilot projects for the use of economic and social development, demonstrating the U.N. system's commitment to development broadly conceived.

In April 1962, the Intergovernmental Committee of the WFP met for the first time to develop the guiding rules for the WFP. While the two-day meeting was taken up with procedural matters, many of the delegates tried to focus on what they saw as the most important aspect of this new program, which was to use food constructively to promote economic and social development in order to create self-sufficient countries, by improving both physical and human capital (FAO 1962). The idea of development and the related paradigm of human capital theory had become central in guiding policy makers' actions.

The WFP proceeded through its three-year experimental period, focusing primarily on emergency assistance, nutrition interventions such as school feeding, and food-for-work programs. As the three-year experimental period for the WFP drew to a close, a number of reports were published by the FAO. These were published under the direction of a U.N. General Assembly resolution, which had asked for reports on various aspects of the World Food Programme in order to determine whether or not to continue the organization.[12] The study on "Food Aid and Education" lays out the justifications for school feeding both in terms of nutritional benefits to children and economic development to the country as whole, discusses a hypothetical school feeding program and the attendant costs, and spends two short sections urging school feeding for post-primary institutions such as secondary and technical schools as well as adult literacy programs. The document makes clear the benefits of school lunch programs while also acknowledging the problems with instituting them:

> The general establishment of school canteens on a world-wide scale can scarcely be envisaged:
>
> a. because the priority devoted to primary teaching varies from one country to another;
> b. because even in those countries which wish to establish general primary education as rapidly as possible, the number of teachers and schoolrooms does not always permit this aim to be achieved;
> c. finally, because for most countries to establish, to equip in however simple a manner, and to maintain a network of canteens in all primary schools must remain a far too costly undertaking. (FAO 1965a, 7)

It is a strangely contradictory document, acknowledging the problems with instituting school feeding programs and yet urging the expansion of those programs.

These same problems were acknowledged in a 1969 report in which the WFP determined that it would be irresponsible to create large-scale feeding programs unless the "financial, technical, logistical, and administrative resources required for their implementation were firmly secured from internal sources and external aid" (Shaw 2001, 102). Thus, the WFP limited the number of places to which it would provide aid. In addition, the yearly variability in donated commodities made planning difficult, especially for projects that require consistent food in order to be successful. While aware of these issues, as the WFP moved out of its experimental years, school feeding projects became more institutionalized and made substantial improvements in the lives of some children. Despite the difficulties laid out in the

1965 and 1969 documents, the WFP worked to implement these programs over the years. By 2013, the World Food Programme had exported the model of school lunch programs into ninety-four developing countries and was feeding 20 million children.

WHY SCHOOL LUNCHES?

Why did the WFP include school lunch programs as a component of its development projects from the beginning of the organization's founding? School lunches are the only specifically named development program in the WFP's founding documents. School lunches were included in the original WFP plans for three reasons. The first was that George McGovern, who had always had a concern for hungry children, used the concern with development in the United Nations at the time as well as the new cognitive paradigm of human capital theory to put school lunch programs on the agenda. Second, school feeding easily fit the WFP's organizational rules. Third, school lunch programs represented a compromise position between those countries that wanted an international food aid organization to provide only emergency aid and those countries that also wanted food aid to stimulate economic and social development. School lunch programs were politically palatable to those countries that wanted a food aid organization to concentrate only on emergency aid. McGovern and Sen negotiated this compromise position, against the backdrop of U.S. agricultural surpluses, by tying their arguments into the ideational context of the time, which emphasized the role of children in development.

The explicit link between human capital and development, popularized through economists' use of human capital theory, encouraged the creation of programs that would encourage children to attend school. Subsidized school lunches, provided by either a state or an international organization, fit these goals of human capital creation and were welcomed for that reason; there was an ideational context of development discourse that focused on humanitarian concerns and human capital creation. The new cognitive paradigm of human capital theory provided Sen and McGovern, as well as policy makers in other countries, a way to conceptualize the kinds of programs that would encourage school attendance as one way to achieve development goals.

In addition to the ideational context, the material factor of U.S. agricultural surpluses and the U.S. food aid regime were important factors in the development of school lunch programs. The U.S. food aid regime was concerned with balancing a domestic need for surplus food disposal against the selling of surplus commodities on international markets, as well as using food aid strategically during the Cold War. Because the United States was the original funder of the program, its agricultural needs were an important consideration as the rules for the organization were created. McGovern was aware of these considerations (Shaw 2001, 9) and created organizational rules that best served the United States and also laid the basis for the inclusion of school lunch programs in the WFP's activities. School feeding fit within the program's goals in several ways. One was that school feeding easily fit the bill of project-oriented food aid, required under the McGovern proposal (FAO 1965b, 50). School feeding was seen as a non-complex project with little room for misapplication or misuse, due to the fact that food is supplied for immediate consumption and with a fairly simple action line between food, school attendance, and smarter government bureaucrats (FAO 1965c, 38). Likewise, school feeding represents additional consumption, which is necessary under the FAO Principles of Surplus Disposal. In other words, school feeding is an opportunity to use food surpluses with no fear of disturbing normal commercial markets (FAO 1965a, 4).

The final step that ensured that school lunches emerged as WFP policy was the way they fulfilled the variety of goals different countries had for providing aid. McGovern and Sen succeeded in creating a compromise policy for countries that saw food aid as useful only for emergency purposes and those that wished to have food aid available for social and economic development. McGovern had to create this compromise with the U.S. policy community and Sen negotiated the same debate within the FAO. School lunches served as a compromise position between these two camps, an obvious good that did not have to be debated endlessly (Luhe 1986, 2:4). There was an "ingenuous belief" at the time that school lunches "must do good to beneficiaries" (Luhe 1986, 2:4). As such, school lunches were more acceptable to those countries and policymakers that wanted a world food organization to focus only on emergency aid. In many ways, school feeding was good public relations for the WFP—people believe intuitively in the benefits of education and nutrition, and a community's parents and politicians usually welcome school feeding programs.

The World Food Programme cemented school feeding as one of their primary programs due to both ideational and material factors. The concern with development and a related cognitive paradigm that linked children's education to national productivity goals worked with the interests of the United States to use its agricultural surpluses in a positive way, as well as allowing the United States to continue to produce those surpluses. In the face of U.S. agricultural interests and surpluses, ideas about children and development influenced decisions about how to handle those pressures. The WFP case indicates that there are a variety of other avenues into which agricultural surplus could be funneled, but the policy decision to create school lunch programs demonstrates the influence of ideas. While ideational factors predominated in helping actors argue for the creation of these programs at the domestic level in Europe and the United States, when moving up the scale to the international level, material factors predominate. This is not to imply that ideational factors were not unimportant, as they certainly were, but simply that ideas around children and development were largely used to justify that which was materially necessary, rather than driving action the way ideas did in other contexts.

6 · CHANGES AND CHALLENGES
Local Food and Cash Transfers

Current state efforts to feed children, led by the WFP and the World Bank, now prioritize partial market solutions to the problem of child hunger. As the WFP has begun phasing out its support for school feeding, driven largely by an increase in food aid emergencies and a new governance structure, most phased-out countries have worked to continue to provide children with food in some way. The WFP and several African countries, including Nigeria, Kenya, and Ghana, bolster local agricultural production through local purchases for school lunch programs (Home-Grown School Feeding), while in much of Latin America school feeding has been replaced by the rise of conditional cash-transfer programs, which give money directly to families in exchange for school attendance. Both of these new models depend on the cognitive paradigm of human capital theory, but layer on post-neoliberal economic theory. The material factor in this case is not agricultural surpluses but rather a lack of them following changes in agricultural policies in the European Union and changes in the policies of the WFP, which has come to ask for monetary aid rather than surplus food.[1] Thus, in the newest phase of school feeding, ideas continue to interact with material factors in ever more complex ways.

PHASING OUT

Although the WFP consistently supported school feeding projects from the 1960s through the 1980s, beginning in the 1990s there was a sudden uptick in situations considered to be emergencies and a subsequent loss of food aid available for development purposes. From 1992 to 1993, the value of foodstuffs used in primary schools dropped from $230 million of donated commodities to $132 million. The decline was even more precipitous the next year when only $73 million of food aid was available for school feeding (Shaw 2001, 85). Suddenly, two-thirds of WFP expenditures began going toward emergency relief, reversing three decades where approximately three-fourths of expenditures had been going toward development. This shift in WFP programming reflected a real escalation in human-caused disasters beginning in the 1980s with events such as the Soviet-Afghanistan War, the African food crisis of the 1980s, and continuing in the 1990s with the dissolution of the Soviet Union, wars in the former Yugoslavia, and the Rwandan genocide (Shaw 2001).

In addition, this shift in the early 1990s reflected a new governing structure that required greater coordination between U.N. bodies. In particular, the WFP and the U.N. High Commissioner for Refugees (UNHCR) became involved in a new working relationship that saw the WFP become the agency charged with feeding refugees (Shaw 2001, 168). The number of displaced people throughout the world numbered 47 million in 1993, up from 11 million in 1980. Since the late 1990s, the number has never fallen below 35 million people in any given year (UNHCR 2014). In the face of these mass flows of displaced people, the World Food Programme has "assumed a major role in providing life-saving food to refugees and displaced persons" (Shaw 2001, 168). As the real numbers of man-made disasters increased and the new governing structure demanded greater attention to the food needs of refugees, development funding fell. Due to these factors, the WFP began to phase out school feeding from certain countries.

Further, in both the EU and the United States, food surpluses have begun to decline as many of the subsidy programs that were enacted in the Great Depression were replaced. In the United States, the Federal Agriculture Improvement and Reform Act of 1996 abandoned the policy of agricultural supply management, which had for so many years produced the surpluses that were often directed into domestic and international food aid (Winders 2009). Similarly, the EU, which implemented agricultural supply management policies when the Common Agricultural Policy was first discussed in 1958, began to decouple subsidies and set budget caps for allowable subsidies in 2003. While the United States and EU continue to produce surplus foods, these policy moves away from a purely productivist orientation has had a real effect on the amount of surplus food available for use in food aid.[2] In addition, in 1996 the EU revised its food aid policy to encourage local food production and correspondingly increased its cash contributions for food aid.[3] These moves by the United States and EU have further encouraged the WFP to phase out school lunch programs.

The WFP phased out their school lunch program in more countries in the 1990s, while even greater numbers of countries were phased out in the 2000s. At this point in time, the WFP has phased school feeding programs out of thirty-seven countries. These countries are listed in table 6.1.

The WFP phases out a country's school lunch program only when a certain socioeconomic standard has been reached, such that the most vulnerable populations are guaranteed access to "basic amenities such as health, education, and food" (World Food Programme 2006, 22). When phasing out, the WFP asks for government commitment and community involvement and promises continued technical support. The WFP leaves a country equipped with experience in managing the programs, infrastructure, an expectation for the program by the community, and the promise of future help.

All but three of the countries from which the WFP has phased out have continued to feed children in some way. In certain countries, particularly in Latin America, in which the WFP used to work, a new program type called conditional cash transfer has been implemented whereby families are given cash, which is assumed will be spent on food, in exchange for their child's attending school. In Africa, countries are moving toward a model that depends on using locally grown foods for the existing school lunch programs. Both programs present radical changes to the model spread by the WFP over the last forty years, which has depended on surplus foods from the developed world. This chapter explores these two different program types, comparing their history and effects while also focusing on the ideational commonality of post-neoliberal economic theory, which is foundational for these changes.

TABLE 6.1 Countries Where the WFP Has Been Phased Out

Albania	Mexico
Antigua and Barbuda	Morocco
Azerbaijan	Namibia
Barbados	Paraguay
Botswana	Peru
Brazil	Philippines
China	Portugal
Comoros	Seychelles
Cyprus	St. Kitts and Nevis
Dominica	St. Lucia
Dominican Republic	Singapore
Ecuador	Swaziland
Equatorial Guinea	Syria
Gabon	Thailand
Guyana	Togo
Iraq	Tonga
Jamaica	Turkey
Jordan	Uruguay
Maritius	

POST-NEOLIBERALISM

Economic policies are the enactment of certain ideas about the relationships between citizens, capital, and the state. Neoliberalism, which became the dominant economic discourse in the 1980s, can be thought of as a utopian project focused on creating favorable conditions for the accumulation of capital (Harvey 2005; Yates and Bakker 2014). The roots of neoliberalism's ideologies can be found in eighteenth-century liberal political theory, which have been reworked such that today this ideology is reflected in the creation of low tax regimes and demands for limited state interference and unimpeded access to markets and vital resources (Hall, Massey, and Rustin 2013). Neoliberalism is reflected in the whole-scale transformation of industry and social services in many regions of the world, particularly Africa and Latin America. In these two regions in particular, which were forced through structural adjustment programs to follow the Washington Consensus reforms, countries in both regions privatized industry and social provision and drastically reduced the role of the state in providing social services (Corboz 2013; Owusu 2003).

In many countries within these regions, a new ideological project has arisen, largely in response to the suffering engendered by the implementation of neoliberal ideas. *Post-neoliberalism* encompasses a wide variety of responses to neoliberalism as the state has sought, often on the heels of left-wing reformers being elected into office, to overcome "the ideological and institutional heritage of neoliberalism" (Yates and Bakker 2014, 64). Post-neoliberalism is not a break from neoliberalism but can be similarly conceived of as a utopian project. However, it contests the hegemony of neoliberalism through a set of practices that re-embed the state in the provision of social services, direct the market toward social concerns, and revive citizenship through a focus on empowerment and participation (Corboz 2013; Yates and Bakker 2014). The post-neoliberal state strives to sustain economic growth while improving the chances of its citizens for equity and social inclusion (Grugel and Riggirozzi 2009). Post-neoliberalism accepts many of the assumptions of neoliberalism but seeks to work with them to produce more socially just outcomes.

Ultimately post-neoliberalism represents new ideas about the relationships among the economy, state, and citizens and is a collection of practices that seek to put these ideas into action. In other words, the cognitive paradigm of post-neoliberalism helps states as they puzzle through their reactions to the effects of neoliberalism. For instance, one of the hallmarks of post-neoliberalism is the inclusion of women and care work as a state concern in marked contrast to the way in which such work was devalued under neoliberalism. Similarly "women-centered approaches to governance" have become a central principle of the post-neoliberal state (Simon-Kumar 2011, 441). Governments in Africa and Latin America, as well as other regions, are enacting post-neoliberalism in a range of policies, particularly by reimagining policies that seek to feed and otherwise care for children, often by focusing on the women who are assumed to care for them.

AFRICA'S HOME-GROWN SCHOOL FEEDING PROGRAMME

Africa has long been one of the primary geographic areas on which the WFP concentrated, and the enthusiasm for school feeding in Africa was such that by 1979, fifty of the fifty-three countries in Africa had some relationship with the WFP's school feeding programs. However, as the WFP began phasing out their programs, this put pressure on African governments to take ownership over their own school feeding programs. In addition, in the early 2000s African leaders, interested in African solutions to African problems, began focusing on agriculture as key to African recovery. School feeding programs fit into leaders' goals for renewing African agriculture, and it was when this connection to local economies was realized that the idea of relying on locally sourced foods for school feeding was developed. In light of this, the New Partnership for African Development (NEPAD) proposed the Home-Grown School Feeding Programme in 2003, while in 2009 the WFP began a new program called Purchase for Progress, which seeks to find local sources for food for WFP programs such as school feeding. These two programs represent a change in the methods by which food for children is provided and rely on local market mechanisms rather than donor aid. However, neither of these programs relies solely on the market for success but rather seeks to better integrate state aid with market mechanisms, one of the hallmarks of post-neoliberalism.

The Home-Grown School Feeding Programme is designed to create markets for local farmers by purchasing local products for use in school feeding projects. Schools' contracts with farmers "include a floor price for their products, lessening their risk" (International Food Policy Research Institute 2004, 2). The program provides market incentives to local farmers, saves money for the school due to the reduced transportation costs, improves student nutrition, and improves the economic welfare of the local community by providing food-processing jobs. This type of program is being experimented with on a local level in places like the United States, United Kingdom, and some other developed countries, but this is the first time this type of program has been attempted on a large scale. The Home-Grown School Feeding Programme has a two-pronged approach to African development: the economic development of local agriculture and human capital development through education. While school feeding programs under the WFP have always focused on the improvement of human capital, less attention has been paid to the positive role they could play in immediate economic development.[4] The attempt to stimulate domestic markets, with state or international aid, is one of the key practices associated with post-neoliberalism.

NEPAD is the development program of the African Union and is focused on good governance and democracy as goals of development, as well as specific economic goals related to improved gross domestic product rates. In particular, NEPAD calls for African solutions to African problems and considers agriculture, human development, the environment, and infrastructure as the priority sectors for increased investment (NEPAD 2001). For each of its priority sectors, NEPAD has developed a Home-Grown Programme plan. The NEPAD Steering Committee created the Comprehensive Agriculture Programme in 2002 with assistance from the FAO. It was quickly endorsed by the African ministers of agriculture and is being implemented. The Comprehensive Agriculture Programme is focused on "extending the area under sustainable land management," creating "reliable water control systems, improving infrastructure and trade-related capacities for market access," increasing the food supply, reducing hunger, and improving agricultural research and technology (NEPAD Secretariat 2002, 1). The Home-Grown Programme fits under the Comprehensive Agriculture Programme's goal of increasing the food supply and reducing hunger.

Plans for the Home-Grown Programme under the Comprehensive Agriculture Programme ask that up to 50 percent of the program cost be borne by international partners. The WFP has emerged as the most prominent partner and provides both technical and financial assistance. In Ghana and Nigeria, WFP support is mostly limited to technical support for setting up programs and governance structures, while in Senegal, Mali, Ethiopia, and Uganda, the WFP has assisted by buying local foods for disbursement in WFP school feeding and other food aid programs (World Food Programme 2007). In all countries, the WFP as well as national governments are working to provide farmers with better information about soil fertility, seed supply, and water management (International Food Policy Research Institute 2004).

The Home-Grown Programme was proposed in 2003, and the first countries did not start to implement the program until 2005. Nigeria, Kenya, and Ghana were some of the first participants and have had mixed results with the program. While Nigeria, which was the first country to begin a program in 2005, initially saw large enrollment increases (*Africa News*, September 18, 2007), the program was suspended two years later. By the beginning of 2010, only one state in Nigeria, Osun, continued to fund the Home-Grown School Feeding Programme (*Africa News*, January 12, 2010). In Kenya, the program has been much more successful as the program has grown to the point that it is now serving over 600,000 children. In Ghana, the program has been very successful and is now serving over 1 million children (Eenhoorn 2011).

The difference in results reflect the differences in state capacity in these countries, as well as other barriers to success such as the potential of corruption, a lack of infrastructure, a lack of capacity in local schools to order and prepare the food, and finally a lack of credibility that the system could work (Tomlinson 2007, 23). One of the other problems with the Home-Grown School Feeding Program has been small farmers' lack of capacity to act as suppliers to the school programs, often related to reasons such as quality control and a lack of ability to transport their goods to the schools.

These issues are likely to be helped by a new WFP program called Purchase for Progress whereby the WFP purchases food from local farmers to use as food aid. Purchase for Progress, or P4P, is finishing a five-year pilot stage in twenty-one countries, two-thirds of which are in sub-Saharan Africa. The main premise of P4P is to "facilitate increased agricultural production and sustained market engagement" (Mitchell and Leturque 2011, 14) by purchasing the foods needed by the WFP in or near the communities in which the aid will be used. This procurement method is aimed at increasing small-scale farmers' production and integration into and engagement with markets. The program is focused on small-scale farmers, often farming less than two hectares, and works to link them into farmers' organizations. These organizations typically work cooperatively to sell many small-scale farmers' goods together. These features make P4P representative of postneoliberal ideology in practice as it works to create sustainable markets that are focused on improving the lives of citizens.

The program depends on a few basic assumptions: that small-scale farmers do not have sufficient access to markets, that this parallel sales mechanism will increase farmer income without increasing consumer prices, and that these purchases will create an incentive for increasing farm production (Aker 2008). If these assumptions are not true, the consequences for local markets could be disastrous. While the program is still in its pilot phase, there have been successes. As of March 2011, when the midterm evaluation of the program was released, the WFP has used P4P to contract 160,000 tons of food commodities (Mitchell and Leturque 2011, xi). In addition, the architects of the program have carefully watched local markets in order to ensure that their purchases do not inflate local food prices. Most importantly for the issue of school feeding, though, is the success of Ethiopia's school feeding program, which, according to the WFP's website, in 2010 began to use P4P foods in thirty-seven schools. Efforts to link P4P directly to school feeding are emerging in all the pilot countries in Africa. The WFP has made this programmatic linkage an important goal and sees P4P as the step toward sustainable, national ownership of school feeding programs.

While Home-Grown School Feeding, supported by programs such as P4P, offers a way toward national control over school feeding rather than a dependence of international organizations or international aid, it also explicitly offers a strategy of gender empowerment. One of the goals of P4P is to create sustained economic benefits for women, as women are responsible for a large proportion of food production and have a large role to play in the food security of their households in rural areas of the developing world. However, there has long been a marked inequality between men and women in their ability to access inputs, transportation, and most importantly, markets (WFP 2011b). The WFP has singled out the P4P program as one that could increase women's market share. The P4P program has established targets for women's participation in farmers' or traders' organizations that include 50 percent women as members in farmers' organizations. This focus on women is also representative of post-neoliberal ideology in practice, as it represents state efforts to include all citizens, women and men, in market activity.

There are of course a number of challenges for improving the livelihoods of women farmers. These include prevalent gender norms, which prevent women from gaining access to land and other resources, the gendered requirement that women take on household and childcare duties in addition to their farming activities, and barriers to their participation—especially leadership in farmers' organizations (WFP Gender Service 2010). Furthermore, there is a division between men's and women's crops, with so-called men's crops such as maize or other cereals often being the ones used in food aid or school feeding (WFP 2011a). Finally, since women, due to custom and law, do not own the land, they do not qualify as smallholder farmers and cannot access the WFP resources available to smallholder farmers.

Despite these constraints, P4P and a focus on Home-Grown School Feeding could enhance the livelihoods of women farmers if certain conditions are met. The WFP works with women farmers who produce crops in which the WFP is interested; these tend to be women who are the head of female-headed households or older women from polygamous marriages (WFP 2011a). To improve the livelihoods of other women, the WFP could expand the types of crops they procure, as women often produce a more diverse basket of crops than their male counterparts in an effort to protect their families from market fluctuations (WFP 2011a). Furthermore, the P4P programs can and should work to promote gender sensitization approaches within their organizations as well as facilitating women's participation in farmers' organizations through the aforementioned participation quota system or through partnerships with other women-focused organizations. Finally, P4P can and should work with other groups within their country contexts that focus on removing the structural barriers to female ownership of land and other resources. These strategies could prove beneficial for women in rural areas in the developing world as well as creating stability for the local school feeding programs.

The WFP has become increasingly invested in local procurement, as well as gender awareness in its programming, and has shown a substantial commitment to these issues. Home-Grown School Feeding provides a model for providing food for children that supports local economies and encourages women to join and reap the benefits of the market economy. In many ways, this model is a return to the original European model whereby school feeding was conceived in part as a support for working women. Under this newer model, women are supported as workers in two ways: both through the provision of school lunches, which leaves them free to work and removes a bit of the childcare burden, and through payment for their creation of food commodities used in the lunches. The focus on women farmers reflects a particular normative framework about the role of women in society as earners that may not reflect the reality of the country-specific normative framework regarding gender, which could prove problematic for the success of this program. Nevertheless, it demonstrates the way in which ideas work in conjunction with one another to promote and create certain policy solutions.

CONDITIONAL CASH TRANSFERS

While the World Food Programme and a number of African countries continue their emphasis on school lunch programs, other countries are adopting a different approach to the twin problems of child malnutrition and school attendance: conditional cash transfer programs (CCTs). Conditional cash transfer programs were begun as localized experiments in Brazil and Mexico in the mid-1990s and have rapidly spread throughout Latin America as well as other parts of the developing world. In South America, all the former Spanish colonies created school feeding programs in at least some of their major cities in the 1930s, but these programs were largely abandoned by the 1960s. The majority of these countries ended up with World Food Programme programs. Those South American countries that created programs did so largely due to the real trials of malnutrition brought on by the Great Depression and the power of workers in the cities. Populist governments at the time, seeking to quell labor unrest (Rothermund 1996, 136; Skidmore and Smith 1997, 48), created "'comedores populares' or popular restaurants . . . for working men and their families" (Scott 1953, 106). These restaurants led easily to the creation of school meal programs in the industrial, urban centers. However, these programs never spread beyond the large cities and were abandoned fairly quickly. While many of these countries depended on WFP aid for several decades, when the WFP began phasing out in that region, these countries turned to conditional cash transfers instead of maintaining school lunch programs.

Conditional cash transfers work by transferring cash to households that meet some particular stated conditions. These conditions are usually health- and/or education-related and can include requirements for medical checkups, vaccinations, and attendance at health talks by mothers, or school attendance for 80 percent of the days in a month. Cash is only provided if certain health or educational behaviors are maintained. The twin goals of the program are to finance immediate consumption as well as "foster investment in human capital" (Das, Quy-Toan, and Ozler 2005, 57). The cash is usually transferred to the mother, rather than the father, under the understanding that mothers are more likely to spend the money on food for the family than fathers would (Bradshaw 2008). CCTs are based on a rational actor assumption that individuals will make the best choices for themselves by weighing costs and benefits (Bassett 2008); when people are given cash, they will make the best choices for themselves on how to spend that money. CCT programs fundamentally respect market principles (Lomeli 2009). CCTs are thought to address a lack of investment in human capital in both the short term by providing nutrition and the long term by requiring certain health and education actions. It is argued that, in effect, CCTs transform cash transfers into human capital subsidies (Maluccio and Flores 2005). The way in which these programs do this, by stimulating the domestic economy through state spending, is a prime example of post-neoliberalism.

Conditional cash transfers are based in the same cognitive paradigm as school lunch programs of human capital theory. In both cases, the thought is that investment into human capital development is one of the best ways to promote national growth, as it is believed that an educated workforce will earn more with subsequent higher tax returns to the state. Conditional cash-transfer programs are related to school lunch programs in three other ways. The first is that in several countries (Mexico, Turkey, and Paraguay), a CCT program explicitly replaced the World Food Programme's school lunch program and is considered an appropriate alternative. Second, in many countries one of the goals of CCTs is to encourage children to attend school, where lunch programs will feed them. Third, and perhaps most important, the fundamental goal of both school lunches and conditional cash transfers is to improve children's nutrition status and encourage families to send their children to school; one of the primary assumptions of most CCT programs is that parents, preferably mothers, will spend the cash that they receive for the child's school attendance on food, thereby meeting both goals. Thus, CCTs represent a new and innovative way to tackle child malnutrition that challenges and supplements the method of school lunches, and is therefore important and useful to analyze alongside of school lunch programs.

The number of countries with a CCT program has grown exponentially since the mid-1990s. In 1997, there were three CCT programs in Brazil, Mexico, and Bangladesh, and in 2008 the World Bank reported that there are CCT programs operating in twenty-nine different countries on every continent except Australia (Fizbein et al. 2009). Some of these programs are quite small or pilot programs at this point, such as in Kenya and Nicaragua, while others are large such as the program in Brazil, which covers 11 million households, or 20 percent of the population. Most of the programs combine health and education objectives, but there are a handful of programs in Brazil, Indonesia, Bangladesh, Cambodia, Yemen, and Pakistan that are focused primarily on educational outcomes (Fizbein et al. 2009). In each of these countries, the targeted population differs: some focus solely on girls, while others focus on secondary schooling and others only on primary schooling. Because CCTs require some level of supply-side inputs such as schools or health centers, CCTs have been more successfully created in the lower-middle-income countries, rather than lower-income countries, but there is a growing interest in the programs around the developing world.

Generally speaking, the programs are successful at reaching the poor and achieving their basic short-term goals such as reducing short-term poverty, decreasing stunting among younger children, improving school attendance, and increasing the use of preventive health services (de la Briere and Rawlings 2006; Fizbein et al. 2009) During the recent financial crisis, a study revealed that those countries that had CCTs were able to respond more quickly to the crisis and at least partially mitigate its effects (Fizbein, Ringold, and Srinivasan 2011). However, the programs have proven less effective at translating these improvements into long-term poverty reduction. In addition, the increase in school enrollment does not necessarily translate into an increase in achievement through testing. This is likely because these types of programs support the demand for social services but do little to support the supply of services such as improved educational facilities or practices (Yaschine and Orozco 2010). In addition, there are likely to be constraints at the household level such as poor parenting or inadequate information (Fizbein et. al. 2009). Furthermore, CCTs work as a retrenchment of welfare, rather than an expansion, in large part because they offer "government an alibi for scaling back provision of public goods" (Lavinas 2013, 38). Although CCTs have been billed as the "magic bullet" of development (Adato and Hoddinott 2010), like any other social program they must be created in an interconnected way with other social and economic developments to be truly magical.

Brazil and Mexico: Origins

The earliest CCT emerged in Brazil, driven by domestic political and economic concerns. While import-substitution industrialization worked to promote rapid industrialization and urbanization in the 1960s and 1970s, these macroeconomic policies were unable to substantially reduce poverty and inequality. Indeed, despite a history of social policy that focused on targeted food subsidy programs, the clientelistic nature of these programs prevented real poverty reduction (Pero and Szerman 2010). The 1988 constitution prioritized social and economic rights but was most effective at fulfilling the right to health, rather than other social rights such as food or education (Hoffman and Bentes 2008). Responding to this situation in 1991, the leftist workers party (PT) proposed a negative income tax program, which was the first time that the government proposed direct cash transfers to the poor in order to create a safety net (Pero and Szerman 2010, 83). In the debates around this proposal, several themes emerged including the criticism that simply providing cash would not work to break the intergenerational cycle of poverty, which, according to human capital theory, is likely to only be broken by education.

While these debates were occurring in the legislature, the Center for Contemporary Brazilian Studies at the University of Brasilia was running a program for faculty and students, led by a man named Cristovam Buarque, to discuss and develop policy ideas. This group came to the conclusion that education was the key to breaking out of poverty, further cementing the strength of human capital theory. After discussing the problems facing parents who must provide clothing and supplies when sending their children to school, this group proposed a scholarship program that would provide aid for poor families on the condition that their children attend school regularly (Sugiyama 2008).

Cristovam Buarque was elected to office in 1995 in the Federal District, and he started the Bolsa Escola program there, while a conditional negative income tax program was started in the City of Campinas. By 1999 there were fifty-eight CCTs, all run at the municipal level. All of these programs had specific eligibility criteria and participants received benefits for one year, at which point they could reapply to the program. The general term for these programs became Bolsa Escola. Their success drew notice at the national level, and in 2001 the National Bolsa Escola Program was created with U.S. $680 million, which was just 0.7 percent of all national social expenditures at the time. The national program standardized eligibility, conditionality, and benefits. It required children to attend school 85 percent of the time and gave R$15 per month for up to three children.

In addition to the National Bolsa Escola Program, there were two other CCT programs that targeted slightly different populations and had slightly different conditionalities. For instance, the Programa de Erradicacao do

Trabalho Infantil, a municipal-level program started in 1996, was targeted at families with working children and aimed to eradicate child labor by improving school attendance with a cash transfer of R$25 per child in rural areas and R$40 in urban areas. The Bolsa Alimentaco, started in 2001, was also aimed at families with very young children. This program promised R$15 per month for up to three children as long as the mothers attended antenatal care and growth monitoring and the children were sent to pre-school or daycare.

In 2002 Lula was elected president from the Workers Party, and one of his goals was to consolidate the various municipal and federal CCT programs into one. He created the Bolsa Familia Program, which includes both poor families with children and the very poor without children. Families are required to send children to school up to the age of fifteen and keep vaccines up to date for children up to age six, and pregnant women must receive antenatal care. In exchange for meeting these conditions, the families are given variable cash amounts based on family composition, up to R$45 a month. The program currently assists 11 million families in Brazil, and it has been shown that one-sixth of the documented fall in the poverty level can be attributed to Bolsa Familia (Pero and Szerman 2010).

While Brazil was the first country to experiment with CCTs, Mexico's model, first called Progressa and now called Oportunidades, has become the model for design, implementation, and evaluation that is followed by most other countries. Like Brazil, Mexico's CCT program was a home-grown affair. Mexico's economic agenda privileged neoliberal solutions, but there was a history of antipoverty programs that sought to achieve equality. The 1988 Salinas presidency focused on the very poor in Mexico. This administration created the Programa Nacional de Solidaridad (PRONASOL), which targeted the poor for income redistribution. This program was easily manipulated by political interests and did not reach the roots of the poverty problem (Cornelius, Craig, and Fox 1994). However, the program arguably set the agenda for a sustained attention to antipoverty policy under the next administration.

When President Ernesto Zedillo took office in 1994, Mexico was in a state of political and economic instability due to a financial crisis. The implementation of NAFTA focused the attention of the government on becoming more competitive through human capital development. Zedillo's social policy sought to improve social services in general but also targeted the poorest of the poor, specifically by developing human capital. Jose Gomez de Leon, the general secretary of the National Population Council, drafted a program that would transfer resources to poor women and require school attendance in return. Building on Gomez de Leon's draft, Progressa was designed by a variety of stakeholders including the ministries of finance, education, social development, and health and included both health and education conditionalities. Progressa provided cash transfers, school scholarships, a basic preventative healthcare package, and nutritional supplements for children below school age and pregnant or lactating women (Yaschine and Orozco 2010). The cash was transferred directly to the women with the assumption that they would use it to purchase food. The program was designed to achieve both short-term and long-term objectives, including the immediate reduction in nutritional deficiencies and the long-term development of human capital.

Mexico has a long history of scrapping the social programs of preceding governments, and when Vicente Fox won election in 2001, as the first non-PRI candidate in over seventy years, there were fears that he would discontinue Progressa. Instead, he not only continued the program but expanded it to urban areas and up to the high school level. He renamed the program Oportunidades and doubled its coverage to 5 million households.

The World Bank

While both the Mexican and Brazilian programs were clearly designed as local responses to the issues of poverty, hunger, and education (Pero and Szerman 2010; Yaschine and Orozco 2010), there was a convergence of this type of policy response with the antipoverty agendas of international banking institutions. In particular, the World Bank began focusing on targeted benefits, transfers, and human capital building in the mid-1990s (Yaschine 1998) and today is one of the largest proponents of and lenders to CCT programs. CCTs fit well with the World Bank's guiding principles on social policy, which emphasize market solutions to social provision, in line with post-neoliberal ideology.

The World Bank prioritizes "macro-economic stability, pro-export policies, and commercial and economic liberalization" (Bonal 2004, 651) as the keys to economic growth and focuses on privatization, deregulation, and a reduction of the public sector. While the bank's main focus is on development policy, it has also been involved with education, antipoverty, and social policy at various levels over the years. There have been changes over time in the World Bank's approach to these policies. Initially, both anti-poverty and education policy were aimed only at increasing the income-earning assets of the poor, while today these policies also focus on social aspects, largely due to the social implications of structural adjustment pro-grams in the 1980s. The bank has evolved from the 1980s, when economic growth was the only perceived solution to poverty, to the 1990s, when eco-nomic and social development were perceived as necessary for poverty reduction, to today, when social development and poverty alleviation are thought to work together to stimulate economic growth (Vetterlein 2007). Although the more recent strategies of the bank focus on the intertwined nature of economic and social policies, the bank's main interests remain in creating strong global markets as per their Articles of Agreement (Bonal 2004). While the bank can plausibly claim to have left behind a strict neo-liberal orientation, it remains focused on market-led economic growth.

The World Bank has long been interested in human capital development and started to include education as a component of development in the 1960s, as human capital theory became popularized. The bank realized that loans for capital improvements were unlikely to be helpful without people who were educated enough to run new factories, build infrastructure, or implement new agricultural techniques (Bonal 2004). In the early years, World Bank education policy was limited to the equivalent of vocational schools, but this changed in the early 1980s as the bank became convinced of the need for primary and academic education as well. Responding to internal incentives, as well as rate-of-return studies that demonstrated the higher rate of return on investments in primary education over second-ary education and secondary education over tertiary education, the bank created the "short education policy menu" in the 1990s. This allowed the bank to make cognitive shortcuts and insist on similar education models across the globe. This use of human capital theory gave the World Bank an economic rationality on which to base education decisions (Bonal 2004). Support for education policy continues to hinge on the ways in which edu-cation is expected to improve a country's economic standing.

While the World Bank has been involved with education policy since the 1960s, the bank has only more recently become overtly involved with social policy. While bank social policy has three strands, including social welfare, social development, and social protection, I concentrate here on social protection, as that is the area under which CCTs fall. Social protection policy in the World Bank emerged in response to the failures of structural adjustment; as net poverty increased in many countries, welfare provision was one of the easily scaled-back state outlays. CCTs are one type of social protection policy used by the World Bank, which generally focuses on targeted investments for the poor or "environmental and social safeguard policies designed to mitigate the potentially harmful effects of bank-funded infrastructure projects" (Hall 2007, 157). CCTs are seen as advantageous for the bank because they are targeted at the poorest and most vulnerable rather than more universally, which the Bank regards as a more effective use of resources, and the loans for CCTs are generally quite large, which incentivizes the portfolio managers who are rewarded based on financial turnover (Hall 2007). In addition, CCTs work well to produce the educational and health benefits in which the bank is also interested.

CCTs are a program type where the goals of social protection and education promotion collide in a productive manner. They work to put cash in the hands of the vulnerable, turning them into consumers and reinforcing market mechanisms for poverty alleviation. In addition, CCTs increase the number of children who receive an education, which, according to human capital theory, will produce economic benefits for the country in the future. Thus, CCTs are a natural fit for the World Bank, as they work within bank-accepted understandings of poverty reduction and human capital development. Both the mechanism by which CCTs operate and the discourse surrounding CCTs align with World Bank goals and principles. CCTs fit the cognitive paradigm of human capital theory and post-neoliberal economic theory that guide the World Bank's decision making around social protection.

COMPARING THE FUTURE(S)

The future of providing food for children is likely to be split between these two models. The move toward local supply chains for school lunches is not only occurring in Africa but in many developed countries with school lunch programs. For instance, the National Farm to School network in the United States emphasizes the use of local foods in school meals. Likewise, the growth of CCTs is likely to continue in the near future, particularly due to the support of the World Bank. These two models have very different assumptions about the best way to assure the nutrition of children and have very different effects on women. However, both programs are driven by similar factors.

In both cases, a lack of global agricultural surpluses can be considered the material factor that contributed to the creation of these new program types. There are fewer supplies available to the WFP as states have rearranged their domestic agricultural priorities and the attendant policies, and are now less likely to have surpluses available for donation. The changing agendas of each international organization have also driven policy making in this area. The WFP is using the surpluses it has for emergency and refugee feeding, while asking for monetary aid rather than food in an effort to lessen the impact of dumping agricultural products on domestic markets, making the use of local foods more necessary. In the case of the World Bank, they have come to recognize the destructive nature of the strictly neoliberal agenda of the past, but they still seek to create market solutions to education and poverty issues. In both cases, this led to the creation of new program types supported by each international organization based on their own internal dynamics.

The underlying ideational factors, which include a link between the cognitive paradigms of human capital theory and post-neoliberal economics, are the same in both cases. The principles of post-neoliberalism include refounding the state around the social sphere, (re)socialization of the market, repoliticization of civil society, and regional market integration (Yates and Bakker 2014, 71). These ideas have created practices that align closely with both Home-Grown School Feeding and conditional cash transfers. Both program types aim to empower women in particular by increasing their participation in the community and/or the economy (repoliticization of civil society). In addition, both program types hope to stimulate domestic markets through redistributive state spending (resocialization of the market). Finally, both of these programs can be understood as resuming or taking on the role of social provision and regulating that provision. This exemplifies the way in which the post-neoliberal state seeks to re-found the state around the social sphere. The political-ideological project of post-neoliberalism has driven the political calculus of leaders who sought to respond to neoliberalism and has resulted in the creation of these two very different programs.

While the programs share the important commonality of a reliance on market mechanisms with state support, there are important differences in the effects of each program type: each has a different impact on the role and future capabilities of women. The turn to local foods empowers women as producers and workers, while conditional cash transfers reify women as caregivers whose primary role is in the home. The two models, which are the likely contenders for the future of providing food to children in the developing world, have very different results for women. Home-Grown School Feeding has the potential to improve conditions for women in those countries that fully embrace and support the important role of women in rural agriculture, while CCTs work to retard the progress of women in those countries. I turn to this development in more detail in the next chapter.

7 · CONCLUSION

Throughout this book, case studies have illustrated how states' choices to support national agriculture interacted with various ideas to create a program type that has taken hold around the world in three distinct phases. In the first phase, as school lunches were created in a handful of European countries, normative frameworks about the role of women, national security, and government responsibility constrained and created opportunities for policy entrepreneurs to advocate for these programs. Second, cognitive paradigms that specified a link between education and national development dominated policy making as school lunches were created as one of the foundational policies of the United Nations' World Food Programme. Third, the cognitive paradigm of post-neoliberal economics motivated decision makers to switch to market-based solutions to child hunger. School lunches as global policy were created largely as a by-product of state activity in other policy areas, notably agricultural policy, education policy, and employment policy. However, the ideas policy makers had about various factors such as the proper role of women, causal theories about the value of educating children, and causal theories about state intervention in the economy worked with these material or institutional factors to influence the creation or lack of creation of school lunch programs.

To surmise that material and ideational factors, on a national and global level, interact to produce social policy has several theoretical and policy implications. For instance, this argument can be applied to current cases of school lunch program creation, where programs are emerging based on new ideas like human rights in India or a restructuring of the gender regimes in Germany and Canada. In addition, the lessons drawn from this history about the interaction between states and families and how states work to construct the role of women suggests that school lunch programs are the embodiment of a new norm, that there is a public responsibility to feed children. The focus on gender in so many of these cases suggests that states have used their policy choices around feeding programs to reinforce women as either carers or as earners, each of which has different implications for the inclusion of women as full citizens. Finally, the history of school lunches suggests scholars must expand their narrow understanding of social policy to include the broad variety of ways in which states intervene to regulate their citizens. They must include in their analysis the ways other types of policy, such as agricultural, economic, or educational policies, can have effects on social policy in particular.

INDIA, GERMANY, AND CANADA

This argument has not only historical but contemporary resonance as countries that have not previously fed children begin to take up the issue. For instance, India created the largest school meals program in the world, regularly feeding 130 million children a day, in 2001. The creation of this program was spurred by both the accumulation of agricultural surpluses due to the Green Revolution and changing ideas about human rights and government responsibility. Tracing the emergence of this program reveals that ideological and material factors continue to interact in the creation of feeding programs.

A program to feed children, the National Programme of Nutritional Support to Primary Education, was drawn up in 1995, largely in an effort to boost support for the National Congress Party. However, the program was never enacted as the Congress Party lost power in the 1996 election. The program remained on the books, however, and would come into being in 2001, when the People's Union for Civil Rights, a national NGO, took a famine case to the Supreme Court. They had taken on the issue after there were widespread starvation deaths in the state of Rajasthan during the droughts of the late 1990s and early 2000s, despite excess grain being stored in government storehouses. They petitioned the court to enforce the food schemes already in place, such as the Mid-Day Meals Scheme from 1995, and to enforce the Famine Code, which allows for the release of grains in times of famine.

In November 2001, the Supreme Court found that there was a right to food, based in the Indian Constitution's right-to-life provisions as well as previous expansive readings of these provisions by the Supreme Court. This decision began a long process of hearings and further orders on the case, which included an order to not only institute the 1995 plan but expand it to include hot meals. The interactive and iterative nature of the legal process between the court and the PUCL worked to change the social conditions in India and led to a populace that demanded the fulfillment of the right to food (Rutledge 2012). In April 2004, the court issued another order—this time ordering the state governments to implement the program by September. The newly elected government, the Progressive Democratic Alliance, did so, creating the revised National Programme of Nutritional Support to Primary Education. Since October 2004, there has been true implementation of the midday meals program. Data from the Supreme Court Commissioners in 2011 indicate that except for the states of Manipur and Delhi, which have meals in only 70 percent of their primary schools, all other states are providing at least 94 percent of their primary children with midday meals.

Material factors, particularly agricultural surpluses, were an important precipitating factor in the creation of this program. India was able to start conceptualizing school feeding programs in 1995 in part because they had achieved agricultural self-sufficiency by the mid-1990s and the court case was inspired by the government grain surpluses. However, most important were ideas about human rights. Human rights were fundamental in the creation of this program, and particularly the Supreme Court's willingness to expand the constitutional right to life to include other rights. Human rights are ideas about how people should be treated by one another, by their government, and by the international community; "the notion of human rights builds on the idea of a shared humanity" (A. Sen 1999, 40). While many states continue to violate their human rights obligations, human rights remain a powerful idea that has been codified by the international community of states. As such, the PUCL was able to take advantage of the material conditions of agricultural surplus and the idea of human rights that had become so central to the Supreme Court's identity in order to press for the creation of a program. The case of India clearly demonstrates the applicability of this argument to understand contemporary efforts to form school feeding programs.

In Canada and Germany, demand has increased for school feeding programs, based largely on changing ideational factors, particularly those about women and poverty. In neither country are material factors a major factor in creating pressure for these programs. In Canada, school meal programs have begun to be created largely as volunteer or charity projects at the local or provincial level. School meals in Canada range from school food cupboards run by teachers to full meal programs with paid staff and community involvement (Hyndman 2000), and a survey by Health Canada indicated that some kind of school feeding goes on in every province or territory. This same survey indicates that volunteers who were concerned about the large number of children coming to school hungry drove most programs. The emergence of these programs correlates precisely with a policy change that revealed large numbers of children living in poverty.

In 1989, child poverty suddenly appeared in the Canadian discourse (Ismael 2006, 41), largely due to the 1989 change in the child benefits. The child benefit system that began in the 1940s had evolved, until 1989, as a "broad-based system that cover[ed] the large majority of families" (Battle 2007, 26); however, in 1989 the tax exemptions were removed and the federal government shifted to an income-tested benefits system. It was at this point that the issue of child poverty was "discovered." An all-party resolution was passed calling for the elimination of child poverty by 2000 and a (re)revised system of child tax benefits in 1992 and again in 1997. With the "discovery of poverty," different organizations have begun both to provide school lunches to children and to pressure the national government to provide those lunches. The issue of child malnutrition must be considered problematic before organizations can even begin to argue for school lunches; if an issue does not exist, it is impossible for organizations to address it. The gendered nature of the Canadian welfare state hid the issue of child poverty, but now the issue of child malnutrition has been revealed and people have begun to organize around this issue specifically. Thus school feeding in Canada has become a possibility as child poverty has emerged as area of concern, and caring for children has become a driving ideational factor in and of itself.

Germany presents a similar case. As we saw earlier, Germany did not create a meal program in the postwar period due to an overwhelming gender ideology that found it best for women to be in the home, rather than at work.

However, pressure is building on the German state to introduce school meals, and several state governments have begun providing meals. This provision of meals has happened more smoothly in eastern parts of the country where school meals were provided as state policy until the dissolution of East Germany in 1990. However, in western parts of the country the creation of school meals is a relatively new endeavor, and depends largely on women moving into the workforce and demanding help from the state to make it easier to fulfill their jobs as both mothers and workers. This change in women's roles is still contested, and that contestation reveals the importance of ideas for both hindering and creating the possibility for meal programs.

The tradition of half-day schools, combined with policy measures and social pressure, have helped keep women out of the workforce in western Germany. Women who hire others to care for their children or take advantage of the few meal programs and all-day school programs that exist are called *rabenmutter,* or raven mother, which connotes a bad mother (Bennhold 2010; *The Economist* 2011). Today 68 percent of German women work, but that number drops to 14 percent of women who have one child and 6 percent who have two children (Bennhold 2010; OECD 2013). While some believe that the lack of family-friendly policies is due to the similarity between some of these programs and communist programs, it is widely understood that conservative attitudes about women's roles and "fear that the social order would collapse" if women worked are to blame for the low numbers of women with children in the workforce (Kunin 2012, 38). However, prompted by labor shortages and slipping educational standards, the labor minister from 2009 to 2013, Ursula von der Leyen, began encouraging the federal states to create all-day schooling with lunch programs in order to encourage women to rejoin the workforce after having children. As programs have been created, the demand for the expansion for these programs has been intense, as women both desire and need employment.

In short, in Germany it is a slowly changing ideology around women's roles that is producing a demand for school lunches, while in Canada new knowledge about child poverty is producing it. Even in the absence of strong material factors, ideational factors are driving these demands for feeding programs. The reforms in these two countries are much less significant than in India, as neither country has created a full-scale feeding program. The absence of agriculture as a factor in these two cases might suggest that these reforms will not be fully realized until there is a substantial agricultural surplus. On the other hand, the broad range of feeding programs in Canada and the support for feeding programs as part of a suite of family-friendly policies in Germany suggest that programs will be created in both countries, even in the absence of the agriculture factor. If this indeed happens, it suggests that the necessity of particular agricultural conditions as a factor in the creation of school lunches might be lessening, particularly as a global norm about the importance of feeding children spreads.

POLICY AND PUBLIC VALUES

Policy simultaneously reflects and creates public values (Pildes 1991). Policy making always carries moral and cultural judgments that reverberate in the lives of those the policy in question is intended to benefit, as well as affecting those the policy is not necessarily intended to benefit. For instance, welfare policy in the United States clearly reflects middle-class norms and expectations about white mothering and rewards those who attempted to meet those expectations while disempowering and punishing those who do not or cannot fulfill those norms, often by virtue of their race (Mink 1994). Similar normative standards are embedded in welfare policy, and particularly family policy, across Europe as well. In the case of school lunches, policy making reflected ideas about the role of the family and the role of the state as well as ideas about the appropriateness of women's employment.

In many ways, the story of school lunches is a story about the changing relationship between the family and its governing institutions, be they the state or another type of organization. At the turn of the century, around the world, it was assumed that the family or close community was responsible for the physical care of their children. Over the last hundred years, that assumption has been reworked. It is now considered the responsibility of both the family and society as a whole, represented in the form of the state or another type of organization, to physically care for children, at least in the matter of food. This represents a fundamental reworking of the role of families and is a surprise considering the pervasive retrenchment of the welfare state in most other areas, wherein families are being asked to reassume responsibilities the government had previously taken on (Pierson 1994; Starke 2006). This suggests that there is something unique about feeding children as compared to other areas of welfare provision.

This change, to government responsibility for what had previously been the province of families, is not an unusual one. The state has been involved in the regulation and legitimation of families for well over the last hundred years, around the world. Population policies, marriage registration requirements, and compulsory education requirements (Mehrotra 1998) are three examples of important and pervasive interventions by the state into the family. Indeed, the governance of the family by the state has a long history: laws dating from the mid-sixteenth century regulate infanticide (Cunningham 2005, 118),[1] Martin Luther began arguing for compulsory education provided by the state in 1530 (Cunningham 2005, 119),[2] and state-run foundling hospitals began to appear in the eighteenth century (Cunningham 2005, 127). While state support for families and children certainly expanded rapidly in the post–World War II period, increased state intervention into families began before World War II in certain parts of the world.

The study of school lunch programs reveals that it is no longer simply the state but also the international community, represented by various international, nongovernmental, and regional organizations, that have taken on a role of intervening in, or at the very least taking some responsibility for the feeding of children. The introduction and widespread adoption of school lunch programs indicates that public values have shifted in favor of this type of intervention into the family, while simultaneously, the ongoing lived experience of families who benefit from this policy continue to shape an understanding that this is now the state's role.

Thus, the creation of school lunches as global policy suggests the emergence of a new norm: a public responsibility to feed children. A norm is a standard of behavior appropriate for an actor with a given identity (Katzenstein 1996, 5), and these assumptions about that behavior are shared by a "collectivity of actors" (Checkel 1999, 83). In other words, a norm exists as a shared assessment about appropriate behavior (Finnemore and Sikkink 1998, 892). Determining whether a norm exists means seeing how a community, society, state, or some collectivity reacts to different behaviors. Norm-breaking behavior produces disapproval or condemnation, while norm-conforming behavior produces praise or no reaction at all if the norm is deeply ingrained (Finnemore and Sikkink 1998, 892). We are, in general, able to know a norm only through indirect evidence, either through the discourse around the subject or through behavioral change.

There are a number of pieces of behavioral and discursive evidence throughout the later chapters of this book that suggest that state responsibility for feeding children is slowly becoming a new norm. This includes both state and international organization behavior. In particular, the number of states that continue school lunch programs after the WFP leaves suggests that states have adopted this norm. While not every one of these countries continued to have a school lunch program, most notably Mexico, Paraguay, and Turkey, every country has continued to feed children in some way. This result suggests a normative commitment to feeding children. In addition to the countries that continue programs after the WFP has left, or countries such as Canada and Germany that are instituting programs (Bennhold 2010; Dorrell 2007), the countries that are adopting conditional cash-transfer programs are further evidence of this new norm. While that might seem counterintuitive, as it is the parents (mothers) doing the actual feeding in CCTs, these programs are based in a logic that parents need help providing the food and that it is the responsibility of another entity to provide the means to that food.

Further, during the last half of 2007 and the first half of 2008, world food security was dramatically threatened by a sudden rise in agricultural prices. This crisis had many causes, including a rise in oil prices, poor climatic conditions, speculation, increased biofuels production, and changing demographic and consumer patterns (UNCTAD 2008). In two countries, Kenya and Cambodia, the World Food Programme had to temporarily suspend the school lunch program as it scrambled to find available foods and money (Harman 2008). While this looks like a setback for this emerging norm, by August 2008 the programs in both countries had been restored due to the decision made by the WFP's executive board in June 2008, which created a new four-year strategic plan emphasizing the use of school lunch programs along with emergency aid and a new warning system (U.N. 2008). At this meeting, the WFP decided to expand school lunch programs to cover children during the summer season in Liberia, Burundi, and Senegal. Thus, while the initial reaction to the crisis meant that WFP programs in a few states were suspended, they have since been restored, and there is a larger commitment from the WFP for school feeding programs now than since the mid-1990s.

These pieces of evidence suggest that the idea that feeding children is no longer only the responsibility of the family is gaining credence in the international system. Children in a majority of states are provided food by some organization other than their family. This trend, which began in the early 1900s, is now well established in many developed and developing countries, as well as the programmatic playbook of important international organizations such as the United Nations and the World Bank. Even developed countries that have not previously had school feeding programs are beginning to feel pressure from domestic actors to institute such a program. Policies that provide food to children, either in schools or through cash to their mothers, promotes the value that there is a public responsibility to feed children.

The idea that there is a new norm related to feeding children is further bolstered by the Social Protection Floors Initiative, which is premised on a number of claims that fit this worldview. This initiative, embodied in ILO Recommendation 202 (2012) and endorsed by the U.N. system, puts forward a human right to social protection, which includes access to basic income as well as basic services. While a number of essential social service areas are covered by Social Protection Floors, those related to food suggest both cash and in-kind transfers in order to fulfill the duty to provide protection to children as well as adults (Cichon, Behrendt, and Wodsak 2011). The idea of social provision is becoming embedded within the existing human rights framework, strengthening it even further. This is additional proof that this norm is taking hold in a global context, as more countries become aware of and agree to this initiative.

A normative commitment to feeding children based on an idea of social provision as a human right contrasts sharply with the previous reasons for these programs, particularly the human capital perspective, which suggested that if the investment did not produce adequate returns, then it would be cancelled. In short, the specific ideas that were instrumental in the creation of the programs have implications for a country's commitment to the program, and that commitment will inevitably be strengthened as the norm of food access as a human right becomes further entrenched. The development of such a norm is particularly surprising in a neoliberal or post-neoliberal global environment, in which much responsibility has been placed back in the hands of families and individuals. However, the strength of the normative and material commitment to these programs by national governments and international organizations suggests that a concern with children has become a motivating factor for most actors, and that these feeding programs are likely to continue.

WOMEN AS CARERS, WOMEN AS EARNERS

Theodore Lowi (1972) calls for in-depth examinations of policies in order to determine how policies affect politics. Certainly school lunches have achieved the particular policy goals of disposing of agricultural surpluses both nationally and globally, and of reducing childhood malnutrition, particularly in the developing world. However, in addition to these goals, school lunches have had both intended and unintended effects on women and the family, and have changed the political calculus for the politics of gender in a way that is similar to the advent of childcare programs. There is a growing literature on gender and policy that considers the unintended effects of policy choices on women on political participation (Mettler 2005; Soss 1999), and gender scholars have always seen the work of the welfare state as at least in part delimiting the boundaries of citizenship for women (O'Connor, Orloff, and Shaver 1999). School lunch programs, operating as both agricultural and social policy, also contain normative expectations, particularly for women and their role as mothers, and have real consequences on women's lives.

For instance, before lunch programs were institutionalized, the expectation in many countries was that children would go home in the middle of the day for a hot lunch. In fact, in the early part of the twentieth century very few schools were built with kitchens or meeting rooms for children to eat together (Hagemann, Jarausch, and Allemann-Ghionada 2011). The expectation that children would go home for lunch and the lack of infrastructure to eat a home-provided lunch at school meant that women were expected to be home in order to provide lunch. If, however, lunch is provided at school or there are places to eat food brought from home, women will be able to work outside the home. In several countries, in the first phase of program development, women were seen as an explicit beneficiary of school lunch programs, and the creation of school lunch programs can be regarded as a boon for women's incorporation into full citizenship, as employment is often the requirement for reaping those benefits (Mettler 1998; Sainsbury 1999; Strach 2007).

The recent adaptations to the World Food Programme's school lunches, which seek to incorporate and support women farmers, and the growth of conditional cash transfers further demonstrate the ways in which decisions about children and food can have consequences for women's lives. In the case of Home-Grown School Feeding, the policy choice affirms women in the role of earners, and works to promote women as full and equal agents in their local economic system. The conditional cash-transfer programs reflect a primary understanding of women as mothers and carers, and the program is structured such that it rewards women for taking on those roles. The different structures of the two programs "play a role in creating social understandings and fostering particular types of social relationship" (Pildes 1991, 940). In each case, very different values about the role of women are reflected and reinforced by the particular policy choice.

CCTs have been conceptualized as being pro-women as the programs put cash into the hands of women and often reward those families who send girls to school with even greater incentives. Certainly these programs can encourage women's agency and provide some measure of empowerment, but studies suggest that the gender focus of these programs simply works to reinforce women in their roles as mothers or housewives rather than truly empowering them. While some studies reveal that women do benefit from these programs and that some mothers benefit from the health checks, family planning, participation in workshops, and increased decision-making powers (Molyneux and Thomson 2011), a study of the conditional cash-transfer program in Nicaragua revealed that there is a reification of traditional gender roles through many components of the program, which include mandatory parenting classes for women but not men, and praise if a woman's child is found to be growing during the mandatory health checks but blame if the child is not (Bradshaw 2008).

CCT programs that are women-centered focus on women's roles at home and as mothers, and leave men out of the programs. In fact, by providing cash instead of food at school, these programs increase the duties for women at home as they are expected to use that cash to purchase and prepare food for their families; there are also new responsibilities and burdens, particularly of a woman's time as she is now expected to do the work of meeting those conditions such as taking children to their appointments (Molyneux and Thomson 2011). This can further contribute to the marginalization of women from traditional economic sectors, which in turn lessens women's economic empowerment. CCTs ultimately contribute to the state regulation of both motherhood and fatherhood, reinforcing women as the carer solely responsible for children's welfare and ignoring men as potential carers and consigning them to a gendered stereotype of shiftless and lazy (Molyneux 2008).

CCTs reflect an era in which we have moved from the feminization of poverty to the feminization of poverty alleviation (Chant 2008). In this conceptualization, women are responsible for meeting the conditions set by the state, which reflects a paternalistic attitude of both program managers and supporters. The trend toward investing in women as the means toward poverty alleviation means treating women like an instrument (Bradshaw 2008) or a policy conduit. Programs therefore don't include components such as vocational training for women or childcare structures that allow women to study, train, or work (Molyneux 2006).

In the latest phase of school feeding, policy choices driven by a cognitive paradigm of post-neoliberal economic theory, filtered through each international organization's procedures and processes, have resulted in very different effects on women and their ability to fully participate in the lives of their communities as citizens. In particular, social citizenship is often conceived of as dependent on equality of access to employment; as Julia O'Connor wrote, "Independence is the key to citizenship and in the democratic welfare state employment is the key to that independence" (1996, 78). Home-Grown School Feeding promotes women as citizens, who have the privileges, duties, and rights of social citizenship precisely because these programs help them attain independence and autonomy. On the other hand, CCTs reduce women's autonomy and make them less able to partake of full social citizenship because these programs remove them from the world of employment. Thus, these policy choices have serious implications not only for the health and nutrition of children in the developing world but for the inclusion of their mothers and other women in the community as full and equal citizens. These effects must be taken seriously by policy makers.

SOCIAL POLICY

School lunch programs involve concentrated state effort to intervene into the lives of families and provide benefits to both children and women; as such, school lunch programs provide an avenue to explore one of the myriad ways in which the state protects its citizens. However, school lunches have traditionally been ignored in social policy studies. This occurs in part because the field of social policy has traditionally been so narrowly defined, but in addition, school lunch programs involve the overlap of a number of policy areas, including agriculture, education and economics, which has made it difficult to fit into one field of study. Future research should focus on expanding our definitions of social policy to include the myriad ways in which states intervene into the lives of their citizens, particularly the lives of families, and that research should concretely examine the ways in which policy fields overlap.

The field of social policy originally coalesced around studying state actions "to reduce economic inequality by providing certain floors on income and services and preventing income loss due to certain risks" (Amenta 2003, 97). This idea of social policy reflects the original efforts of the state to make the lives of their citizens better; it reflects the purposes of the original welfare states. As such, academics were simply studying what occurred. However, this definition, with its emphasis entirely on the working man, did much to obscure from study other ways in which the state made efforts to improve the lives of its citizens, especially children or women. More recent work has begun to examine these areas; in particular, feminist analyses of social policy have contributed greatly to understanding the effects of women's social movements on the emergence of policy (Kenney 2003), as well as how the institutions of the state either constrain or create opportunity for women (Ungerson and Kember 1997). Despite the work of feminist theorists, the theoretical apparatuses established for explaining one type of social policy are weak for explaining other types of social policy. In particular, theoretical explanations for policy that affects children are far behind efforts to explain other types of policy.

This project suggests that we must broaden our definitions of social policy. More recent work questions the fundamental definition of social policy and expands that definition to consider public spending on the welfare of citizens (Amenta, Bonastia, and Caren 2001, 213). These efforts are a move in the right direction. A broader definition is necessary to properly assess the variety of policies that currently affect people around the world. A broader definition must also take into consideration the wide variety of organizations through which social policy is now effected, such as international organizations, nongovernmental organizations, and regional organizations.

It is likely that theory will have to develop as well; current theories will not necessarily be able to explain social polices included under a broader definition. For example, a social policy that primarily affects children is unlikely to be explained by conventional theories designed to explain income protections. In particular, work that focuses on tracing the causal arrows between material factors and ideas in the creation of a more broadly defined social policy will likely provide increased insight into our understanding of policy creation and implementation.

Furthermore, it is important to consider the ways in which policies in areas other than social policy might affect social policy itself. In the case of school lunch programs, the primary concerns were with agricultural, economic, and education policy: the decisions made in these policy areas had very real effects on the creation of the particular programs. It is not only that policies have effects that their makers did not anticipate, but that policy overlaps must be taken into consideration. It is necessary to place social policy in the context of the broad range of national and international policy choices. Future research could usefully focus on a network approach to analyzing policy.

CONCLUSION

The history of school lunches is a story of policy makers' choices as they balanced the relationship between food and family. This global history of school lunches has examined the interconnections between the cultural, political, economic, and global dimensions of food production and food provision and provides insight into the fight against global hunger. Agricultural (over)production was originally driven by concrete political needs to please farm constituencies and protect national populations in case of war, but it has led to polarizing environmental, economic, and political effects as well as a necessary and well-liked social program around the world.

School lunch programs are not a magic bullet for poverty, but they are an important tool in the arsenal for fighting poverty. Particularly when used in conjunction with other poverty-alleviation programs and infrastructure-strengthening measures, school feeding has been used successfully in a number of countries to help children. One of the problems with school feeding programs is that they were largely created, at least originally, not as a coordinated response to child poverty and malnutrition but as a response to agricultural surpluses and country concerns with factors such as national security and/or women's employment. As these programs have become an integral part of the safety net in many states, the goals and methods to achieve those goals have changed slowly. This suggests that there is room for improvement in the construction and delivery of nutrition interventions.

Despite the necessary critiques of school feeding programs, these programs are a positive step in global efforts to reduce child hunger. Due to the work of governments, international organizations, and nongovernmental organizations, the numbers of hungry children have been reduced in both developed and developing countries, particularly in the last ten years. However, many children are still malnourished. Out of the 1.9 billion children in the developing world, 100 million of them are still malnourished. More work must be done. School lunch programs, which do reduce short-term hunger, are one of several concrete actions that can reduce hunger and improve the human capital of a country.

APPENDIX
Data and Methods

DATA COLLECTION

In order to analyze the emergence of school lunch programs as global social policy, it was necessary to find out the dates at which these programs emerged in various countries. First I gathered information from the 2004, 2005, and 2006 World Food Programme School Feeding Reports. I then updated the data following the publication of the World Food Programme's 2013 *State of School Feeding Worldwide.* I also used a book published by the FAO in 1953, *School Feeding: Its Contribution to Child Nutrition.* In addition, I searched the State Parties Reports to the UN Convention on the Rights of the Child for information related to child feeding programs. For countries for which I still did not have information, I e-mailed their embassy in the United States asking for any information on school lunch programs. I received a surprisingly high response rate to these e-mails. Some of these e-mails directed me to contact other personnel and I did that. Finally, I used the Internet to access government documents and World Food Programme Reports to fill in the gaps as well as communicating with World Food Programme staff through e-mails and in person in Rome.

The global survey of school lunch programs shows that out of 185 countries surveyed,[1] 151 take responsibility for feeding children at school, either by providing a school lunch program themselves, depending on the World Food Programme or an NGO for lunches, or by providing conditional cash transfers for school attendance. Thirty-four countries provide no lunch program at all; these countries are split between countries that either structure their school day so that children are not at school during lunch or allow school canteens, whereby companies sell food on school grounds or, more commonly, just outside of the school. Very few countries leave the responsibility for lunch provision solely in the family's hands. Listed in table A.1 are those countries that do not provide school lunches.

TABLE A.1 Countries without School Meal Programs

Australia	Iceland	Malta	Saudi Arabia
Austria	Kosovo	Mexico (CCT)	Solomon Islands
Azerbaijan	Krgyz Republic	Monaco	Switzerland
Bahrain	Latvia	Netherlands	Tunisia
Belarus	Lebanon	New Zealand	Turkey (CCT)
Belgium	Libya	Norway	Turkmenistan
Canada	Lichtenstein	Papua New Guinea	United Arab Emirates
Germany	Luxembourg	Qatar	
Greece	Maldives	Samoa	

In the 151 countries that have school lunch programs, the school lunches are administered and provided in different ways. This information is summarized in table A.2. Often the funding agencies overlap, as governments, the WFP, and various NGOs work together to provide school meals. Just as conditional cash transfer programs and school lunch programs coexist, so do World Food Programme–provided programs and NGO-provided programs. In many cases, each organization funds different parts of the program. Less often, but occasionally, the World Food Programme is still working with a government on some aspect of its school lunch program. For these reasons, the total number of administering agencies shown in the table is greater than the 151 total school lunch programs. It's important to note that the numbers change yearly as the WFP and other NGOs phase out of countries or add countries, and as national governments take control of their own programs.

TABLE A.2 Programs by Funding Agency

Funding/Administering Agency	
Government	124
World Food Programme	61
Nongovernmental Organizations	32

Table A.3 indicates those countries in which the World Food Programme has ever been active. I do not have dates for all the World Food Programme countries—these countries are listed in the World Food Programme's Global School Feeding Reports but did not show up in archival searches at the WFP library. This could indicate that the World Food Programme began its involvement with these countries only recently, in a period that the archives do not cover.

TABLE A.3 Countries with Which the WFP Has Been Involved

Afghanistan—1964	Jordan—1977
Albania	Kenya—1979
Algeria—1968	Lao PDR
Angola—1974	Lebanon—1969
Armenia	Lesotho—1965
Bangladesh—2001	Liberia—1970
Barbados—1966	Madagascar—1968
Benin—1975	Malawi—1971
Bhutan—1974	Mali
Bolivia—1987	Mauritania—1963
Botswana—1966	Mauritius—1969
Burkina Faso	Morocco—1964
Burundi—1969	Mozambique—1979
Cambodia	Myanmar
Cameroon—1972	Namibia—1992
Cape Verde—1977	Nepal—1972
Central African Republic—1973	Nicaragua
Chad—1963	Niger—1975
China—1968	Pakistan
Colombia	Paraguay—1970
Comoros—1976	Phillipines—1977
Congo, Democratic Republic	Portugal—1976
Congo, Republic—1969	Russia
Côte d'Ivoire—1968	Rwanda—1965

(continued)

TABLE A.3 Countries with Which the WFP Has Been Involved *(continued)*

Cuba—1978	São Tomé—1977
Cyprus—1968	Senegal—1970
Djibouti—1990	Sierra Leone
Dominican Republic—1994	Singapore—1973
Ecuador—1990	Somalia—1970
Egypt—1980	Sri Lanka
El Salvador—1983	St. Lucia—1983
Equatorial Guinea—1970	St. Vincent—1982
Eritrea	Sudan—1969
Ethiopia—1992	Swaziland—1970
Gambia, The—1970	Syrian Arab Republic—1980
Georgia	Tajikistan
Ghana	Tanzania
Guatemala—1983	Timor-Leste
Guinea—1964	Togo—1964
Guinea-Bissau—1976	Tunisia—1988
Guyana—1990	Uganda
Haiti—1990	United Arab Emirates—1971
India—1975	Uruguay—1977
Indonesia	Yemen—1971
Iran	Zambia—1967
Iraq—1968	Zimbabwe
Jamaica—1984	

Table A.4 includes those countries that created or took over their own program, and the year in which that occurred. I have put in parentheses programs that had already been created but suffered cutbacks or had to be taken over by the WFP and then were reinitiated; for example, Argentina initiated a program in 1932, disbanded the program in the 1960s, and then reinitiated a program in 2004. Likewise, Russia started a program in 1937 as the Soviet Union but today depends on the WFP for school lunches. There are a few countries for which I was unable to find a reliable start date for the program, although I am certain that these countries have school lunch programs.

TABLE A.4 Government-Run Programs by Start Date, as of 2013

Country	Start Date	Country	Start Date
Antigua and Barbuda	2005	Kuwait	1954
Argentina	1932 (2001)	Lithuania	1997
Bahamas	1980	Malaysia	1945
Bangladesh	1993	Mauritius	2006
Barbados	1963	Moldova	2007
Belize	1999	Mongolia	2007
Bermuda		Montenegro	2002
Bolivia	1936	Morocco	2006
Botswana	1966 (1997)	Namibia	1997
Brazil	1985	Nigeria	2002 (2005)
Brunei Darussalam	mid-1940s	Peru	1936 (2005)
Chile	1940	Philippines	2003
Colombia	1935	Poland	1947
Costa Rica	1988	Portugal	1948
Cuba	1946	Romania	1947–48
Cyprus	1996	Russia	1937
Czech Republic	2004	Seychelles	mid-1990s
Denmark	1902	Singapore	1996
Dominica	2006	Slovak Republic	
Ecuador	1938 (1980)	Slovenia	
Egypt	1942 (1995)	South Africa	1994
Equatorial Guinea	2006	South Korea	1998
Estonia	2000	Spain	mid-1940s
Finland	1948	Sri Lanka	1940s
France	1932	St. Kitts and Nevis	1996
Gabon	2006	St. Lucia	1996
Grenada	1980	Suriname	mid-1990s
Guatemala	1993	Swaziland	1992
Guyana	1993	Sweden	1946
Honduras	2003	Syria	2006
Hungary	1949	Thailand	2005

(continued)

Country	Start Date	Country	Start Date
India	2001	Togo	2006
Ireland	1930/31	Tonga	1996
Israel	1950 (2005)	Trinidad and Tobago	mid-1990s
Italy	1953	United Kingdom	1906 (1944)
Jamaica	1926 (1996)	United States	1946
Japan	1946	Uruguay	1931 (1991)
Jordan	2006	Venezuela	1940s
Kazakhstan	1995		

METHODOLOGY

Because I am interested in establishing the causal process by which school lunch programs emerge, I work within the tradition of comparative historical analysis. *Comparative historical analysis* offers "historically grounded explanations of large-scale and substantively important outcomes" (Mahoney and Rueschemeyer 2003, 4). Comparative historical analysis has often been used in work on the welfare state, and this project fits within this tradition. Like others within this research tradition, I am not seeking the creation of new universalizable knowledge but rather a causal explanation of a particular phenomenon; I do attempt to generalize "across multiple instances of [the] phenomenon under investigation" (Skocpol 2003, 412). I work to do this by paying attention to historical processes and temporal sequences and by relying on systematic comparisons. The use of comparison is central to this research tradition, and I make particular use of systematic comparisons in the chapter on Europe. In that chapter, I am able to explore the different causal effects on variables in different contexts, engaging in contextualized comparison (Locke and Thelen 1995) to make my analysis.

I continue my intensive focus on a small number of cases in the chapters on the United States and the World Food Programme and explicitly use process tracing in those chapters. Process tracing as a method uses archives, primary sources such as newspapers and websites, interviews, and secondary sources. The researcher uses these sources to see whether the causal processes a theory hypothesizes or implies in a case is in evidence in the sequence and values of the intervening variables in that case (George and Bennett 2005). In general, the method of process tracing explores the "chain of events by which initial case conditions are translated into case outcomes" (Van Evera 1997, 64–65). For process tracing to be persuasive, one must tell a holistic story, have limited breaks in the causal narrative, and have high-quality evidence from primary and secondary sources. Process tracing allows me to gain inference from within the case rather than from comparison across case; within-case analysis increases access to a wider variety of variables, providing for more nuanced theory development. I can then use the inferences gained in each case to construct my argument in a comparative manner.

It is through these contextualized comparisons of states and international organizations that I am able to advance a causal explanation for the emergence of school lunch programs as global social policy. I fuse both theory and history in these comparisons to articulate an argument that pays close attention to temporal processes; a focus on change over time is central to comparative historical analysis and central to my analysis here (Pierson 2000; Skocpol 2003; Thelen 1999). My focus on causal analysis, temporal processes, and contextualized comparisons puts this work squarely within the tradition of comparative historical analysis.

NOTES

CHAPTER 2   HUNGER, EDUCATION, AND AGRICULTURE

1 Voluntary Guidelines to Support the Progressive Realization of the Right to Adequate Food in the Context of National Food Security, Report of the Thirtieth Session of the Committee on World Food Security (CFS), Supplement, FAO Doc. CL 127/10-Sup. 1, Annex 1 (2004).

2 These countries are Bangladesh, Brazil, Colombia, the Congo, Cuba, Ecuador, Ethiopia, Guatemala, Haiti, India, Islamic Republic of Iran, Malawi, Nicaragua, Nigeria, Paraguay, Pakistan, South Africa, Sri Lanka, Uganda, and Ukraine (FAO).

3 Geneva Declaration of the Rights of the Child of 1924, adopted September 26, 1924, League of Nations O.J. Spec. Supp. 21, at 43 (1924).

4 Declaration of the Rights of the Child, G.A. res 1386 (XIV) 14 U.N. GAOR Supp. (No. 16) at 19, U.N. Doc A/4354 (1959).

5 Convention on the Rights of the Child, GA res 44/25, annex, 44 U.N. GAOR Supp. (No. 49) at 167 U.N. DOC A/44/49 (1989) entered into force September 2, 1990.

6 This has changed recently with the 2010 Child Nutrition Act, which now requires schools to offer a vegetarian option.

7 These eighteen countries are: Bhutan, Cote d'Ivoire, Democratic Republic of Congo, Ethiopia, Gabon, Guinea-Bissau, Malawi, Malaysia, Maldives, Mozambique, Myanmar, Oman, Pakistan, Sierra Leone, Somalia, Sudan, Tanzania, and Zimbabwe.

CHAPTER 3   THE FIRST WAVE IN EUROPE

1 While Esping-Anderson considered and then rejected the idea of a Mediterranean welfare regime, many other scholars have found support for this as a distinctive regime type, which is why I include it here. For example: Flaquer 2000; Gal 2009; Kääriäinen and Lehtonen 2006; Naldini 2003.

2 While data availability varied by state, there was no data at all available for Finland and Portugal as they were not included in the 1957 USDA report and I could not find secondary data in English for either country.

3 Other estimates suggest that only one out nine recruits was healthy enough to serve (Passmore and Harris 2004).

4 An attempt to provide school meals through the Poor Law, passed in 1905, was declared a failure after only one year. Children were simply not fed. The failure was largely blamed on the conflicting missions of the local education authorities who wanted to see as many children fed as possible and the poor guardians who wanted to pay to feed as few children as possible.

CHAPTER 4   THE UNITED STATES

1 By 1937, fifteen states had done this.

2 At the time this agency was called the Federal Surplus Relief Corporation and was created as part of the 1933 Agricultural Adjustment Act.

3 In fact, the connection between security and school lunches was made again during the Cold War (Smith 2012) and as recently as 2010 when a group of retired military generals advocated for healthier school lunches due to obesity in recruits (Mission: Readiness 2010).

4 The Marsh Report was akin to the Beveridge Report in the United Kingdom and envisioned a comprehensive system of social welfare.

CHAPTER 5   THE SECOND WAVE

1 This number is higher than what I count in my survey of school lunch programs and is explained by the fact that the WFP includes preschool feeding programs in its calculations while I do not.

2 This is not true for all countries; for instance, Portugal had WFP support for just one year.

3 There are interesting regional differences as to when the WFP became involved in different countries. The WFP began programs in Africa, and particularly sub-Saharan Africa, almost immediately, as well as in Asian countries. The majority of the programs started in the 1960s and early 1970s are largely based in those two regions. It was not until the late 1970s and 1980s that the WFP became involved with school feeding projects in Central America, and the few programs that were started in the 1990s were in Djibouti, Ethiopia, Guyana, Haiti, and Namibia. These first four countries are particularly poor and likely lacked the ability to provide the infrastructure funding the WFP requires for a school meal program until the 1990s. Namibia did not achieve independence until 1990, which is likely why it acquired a program in the early 1990s.

4 I focus almost entirely in this history on U.S. food aid programs. This is not to suggest that other countries did not have food aid programs, as some certainly did, but they worked primarily within colonial empires rather than being more truly international.

5 This allowed countries with insufficient foreign exchange to purchase U.S. agricultural products, which they then sold through normal market channels, much like the Marshall Plan. The United States either grants or loans back about 80 percent of the currency for specified projects; these projects are usually related to economic development. The United States uses the remaining 20 percent for such activities as developing overseas commercial markets for U.S. food and fiber.

6 USAID, "The History of American Food Aid," http://www.usaid.gov/our_work/humanitarian_assistance/ffp/50th/history.html.

7 A new title, Title IV, was added that allowed countries to buy U.S. commodities on loan and pay for them in dollars on a long-term payment plan.

8 The other senators on the subcommittee included Fulbright (Arkansas), Aiken (Vermont), Capehart (Indiana), and Sparkman (Alabama).

9 Fiber such as cotton and wool are considered agricultural products and are affected by the same trade rules.

10 This was the resolution Eisenhower had sought permission for in August 1960, detailed in Senate Report No. 1922.

11 Sen in his autobiography largely takes the credit for the development of the World Food Programme.

12 The topics of the other studies are "The Linking of Food Aid with Other Aid," "Operational and Administrative Problems of Food Aid," and "The Demand for Food and Conditions Governing Food Aid during Development."

CHAPTER 6   CHANGES AND CHALLENGES

1 With the prominent exception of the United States, most countries have complied with the WFP's decision to switch to monetary aid.

2 It should be noted that food surpluses are dependent on both growing conditions and market prices with the result that there have been some years where bumper crops have produced surpluses and others where low market prices have encouraged dumping surpluses on the market.

3 This is different from the United States, which is required by law to supply 75 percent of its non-emergency food aid as in-kind donations.

4 Attention has certainly been paid to the negative role these programs could have in economic development. Critics point to the way in which U.S. surplus foods as food aid can lead to the depression of local agricultural prices.

CHAPTER 7   CONCLUSION

1 Countries that passed laws punishing infanticide included France (1556), England (1624), Sweden (1627), Württemberg (1658), Denmark (1683), Scotland (1690), and Bavaria (1751).

2 Compulsory education did not pick up with any real speed until the late eighteenth and early nineteen centuries.

APPENDIX

1 The 2013 WFP School Feeding Report surveyed only 153 countries, so these numbers are slightly different from its results. In addition, WFP included countries that have canteens but do not have nationally subsidized school lunch programs.

REFERENCES

Abel-Smith, Brian. 1992. "The Beveridge Report: Its Origins and Outcomes." *International Social Security Review* 45: 5–16.

Adato, Michell, and John Hoddintott. 2010. "Conditional Cash Transfer Programs: A 'Magic Bullet'?" In *Conditional Cash Transfers in Latin America*, edited by Mitchell Adato and John Hoddinott, 3–25. Baltimore: John Hopkins University Press.

Aker, Jenny. 2008. "Does Digital Divide or Provide? The Impact of Cell Phones on Grain Markets in Niger." Center for Global Development Working Paper 154.

Amenta, Edwin. 2003. "What We Know About the Development of Social Policy: Comparative and Historical Research in a Comparative and Historical Perspective." In *Comparative Historical Analysis in the Social Sciences*, edited by James Mahoney and Dietrich Rueschemeyer, 91–130. New York: Cambridge University Press.

Amenta, Edwin, Chris Bonastia, and Neal Caren. 2001. "U.S. Social Policy in Comparative and Historical Perspective: Concepts, Images, Arguments, and Research Strategies." *Annual Review of Sociology* 27: 213–34.

Anderson, Kym. 2006. "Reducing Distortions to Agricultural Incentives: Progress, Pitfalls, and Prospects." World Bank Policy Research Working Paper 4092.

Andresen, Astri, and Kari Tove Elvbakken. 2007. "From Poor Law Society to the Welfare State: School Meals in Norway, 1890s–1950s." *Journal of Epidemiology and Community Health* 61: 374–77.

Archard, David. 2004. *Children: Rights and Childhood.* 2nd ed. London: Routledge.

Arts, Wil, and John Gelissen. 2002. "Three Worlds of Welfare Capitalism or More? A State of the Art Report." *Journal of European Social Policy* 12: 137–58.

———. 2010 "Models of the Welfare State." In *The Oxford Handbook of the Welfare State*, edited by Francis G. Castles, Stephan Leibfried, Jane Lewis, Herbert Obinger and Christopher Pierson, 569–83. Oxford: Oxford University Press.

Bassett, Lucy. 2008. "Can Conditional Cash Transfer Programs Play a Greater Role in Reducing Child Undernutrition?" World Bank Discussion Paper no. 0835.

Battle, Ken. 2007. "Child Poverty: the Evolution and Impact of Child Benefits." In *A Question of Commitment: Children's Rights in Canada*, edited by R. Brian Howe and Katherine Covell, 21–44. Ontario: Wilfred Laurier University Press.

Becker, Gary S. 2009. *Human Capital: A Theoretical and Empirical Analysis, with Special Reference to Education.* Chicago: University of Chicago Press.

Beito, David. 2000. *From Mutual Aid to the Welfare State: Fraternal Societies and Social Services, 1890–1967.* Chapel Hill: University of North Carolina Press.

Beland, Daniel. 2005. "Ideas and Social Policy: An Institutionalist Perspective," *Social Policy and Administration* 39, no. 2: 1–18.

Bendix, Reinhard. 1977. *Nation-Building and Citizenship: Studies of Our Changing Social Order*. Berkeley: University of California Press.

Bennhold, Katrin. 2010. "In Germany, a Traditional Falls, and Women Rise." *New York Times*, January 17.

Berman, Sheri. 1998. *The Social Democratic Moment: Ideas and Politics in the Making of Interwar Europe*. Cambridge, MA: Harvard University Press.

Beveridge, William Henry. 1942. *Social Insurance and Allied Services: Beveridge Report London:* HM Stationery Office.

Blau, Judith. 1996. "The Toggle Switch of Institutions: Religion and Art in the U.S. in the Nineteenth and Early Twentieth Centuries." *Social Forces* 74, no. 4: 1159–77.

Blaug, Mark. 1976. "The Empirical Status of Human Capital Theory: A Slightly Jaundiced Survey." *Journal of Economic Literature* 14, no. 3: 827–55.

Bleich, Erik. 2002. "Integrating Ideas in Policy-Making Analysis: Frames and Race Policies in Britain and France." *Comparative Political Studies* 35, no. 9: 1054–76.

Bock, Gisela. 1991. "Antinatalism, Maternity, and Paternity in National Socialist Racism." In *Maternity and Gender Policies: Women and the Rise of the European Welfare States, 1880s–1950s,* edited by Gisela Bock and Pat Thane, 233–55. New York: Routledge.

Boli, John, Francisco Ramirez, and John W. Meyer. 1985. "Explaining the Origins and Expansion of Mass Education." *Comparative Education Review* 29, no. 2: 145–70.

Boli, John, and George Thomas. 1999. *Constructing World Culture: International Non-Governmental Organizations since 1875*. Stanford, CA: Stanford University Press.

Bonal, Xavier. 2004. "Is the World Bank Education Policy Adequate for Fighting Poverty? Some Evidence from Latin America." *International Journal of Educational Development* 24: 649–66.

Bradshaw, Sarah, with Ana Quiros Viquez. 2008. "Women Beneficiaries or Women Bearing the Cost? A Gendered Analysis of the *Red de Proteccion Social* in Nicaragua." *Development and Change* 39, no. 5: 823–44.

Britnell, George E., and Vernon Clifford Fowke. 1962. *Canadian Agriculture in War and Peace, 1935–1950*. Stanford, CA: Stanford University Press.

Broehl, Wayne G., Jr. 1992. *Cargill: Trading the World's Grain*. Hanover, NH: University Press of New England.

Bryant, Louise. 1913. *School Feeding: Its History and Practice at Home and Abroad*. Philadelphia: J. B. Lippincott Company.

Bulkley, M. E. 1914. *The Feeding of School Children*. London: G. Bell and Sons.

Buzan, Barry, Ole Waever, and Japp de Wilde. 1998. *Security: A New Framework for Analysis*. Boulder, CO: Lynne Reinner.

Campbell, John. 1998. "Institutional Analysis and the Role of Ideas in Political Economy." *Theory and Society* 27, no. 3: 377–409.

———. 2002. "Ideas, Politics, and Public Policy." *Annual Review of Sociology* 28: 21–38.

Chant, Sylvia. 2008. "The 'Feminisation of Poverty' and the 'Feminisation' of Anti-Poverty Programmes: Room for Revision." *Journal of Development Studies* 44, no. 2: 165–97.

Checkel, Jeffrey T. 1999. "Norms, Institutions, and National Identity in Contemporary Europe." *International Studies Quarterly* 43: 83–114.

Chicago Daily Tribune. 1902. "Balk at School Lunches." March 15.

———. 1916. "Take Over School Lunches." March 23.

———. 1921a. "School Lunches Drive Students to Open Revolt." October 27.

———. 1921b. "School Lunches Plan Draws Fire of Women's Club." October 30.

———. 1925. "Children's Lunch Box Is Too Often Filled with Odds and Ends." December 26.

Cichon, Michael, Christina Behrendt, and Veronika Wodsak. 2011. "The U.N. Social Protection Floor Initiative: Moving Forward with the Extension of Social Security." *Internationale Politik und Gesellschaft* 32: 32–50.

Clapp, Jennifer. 2012. *Hunger in the Balance: The New Politics of International Food Aid.* Ithaca, NY: Cornell University Press.

Clark, F. Le Gros. 1948. *Social History of School Meals.* London: London Council of Social Service.

Cohen, Abby J. 1996. "A Brief History of Federal Financing for Child Care in the United States." *The Future of Children* 6, no. 2: 26–40.

Congressional Record. 1946a. February 19.

———. 1946b. February 26.

———. 1956. February 19.

Corboz, Julienne. 2013. "Third-Way Neoliberalism and Conditional Cash Transfers: The Paradoxes of Empowerment, Participation, and Self-Help among Poor Uruguayan Women." *Australian Journal of Anthropology* 24: 64–80.

Cornelius, Wayne, Ann Craig, and Jonathan Fox, eds. 1994. *Transforming State-Society Relations in Mexico: The National Solidarity Strategy.* La Jolla: University of California San Diego, Center for U.S.-Mexican Studies.

Costa, Dora L. 2000. "From Mill Town to Board Room: The Rise of Women's Paid Labor." *Journal of Economic Perspectives* 14: 101–22.

Cunningham, Hugh. 2005. *Children and Childhood in Western Society Since 1500.* 2nd ed. London: Pearson Education Limited.

Das, Jishnu, Quy-Toan Do, and Berk Ozler. 2005. "Reassessing Conditional Cash Transfer Programs." *World Bank Research Observer* 20: 57–80.

Davies, Steve. 2005. *School Meals, Markets, and Quality.* Cardiff: UNISON.

de la Briere, Benedicte, and Laura B. Rawlings. 2006. "Examining Conditional Cash Transfer Programs: A Role for Increased Social Inclusion?" Washington, DC: World Bank.

Donnelly, Jack. 2003. *Universal Human Rights In Theory and Practice.* 2nd ed. Ithaca, NY: Cornell University Press.

Dorrell, Kathryn. 2007. "Why Canada Needs a National School Food Program." *Canadian Living*.

Dreze, Jean, and Amartya Sen. 1989. *Hunger and Public Action*. Oxford: Oxford University Press.

Eastwood, Jonathan. 2005. "The Role of Ideas in Weber's Theory of Interests." *Critical Review* 17: 89–100.

The Economist. 2011. "Baby Blues: A Juggler's Guide to Having It All." November.

Eenhorn, Hans. 2011. "Championing Homegrown School Feeding." *'AgriCultures Network*. http://www.agricutluresnetwork.org/news/hans-eenhoorn. Accessed December 2, 2011.

Eide, Wenche Barth, and Uwe Kracht. 2005. *Food and Human Rights in Development*. Vol. 1. *Legal and Institutional Dimensions and Selected Topics*. Oxford: intersentia.

Esping-Anderson, Gosta. 1990. *The Three Worlds of Welfare Capitalism*. Princeton, NJ: Princeton University Press.

Evans, Peter B., Dietrich Rueschemeyer, and Theda Skocpol, eds. 1985. *Bringing the State Back In*. Cambridge: Cambridge University Press.

FAO. 1946. "World Food Proposals: Why They Were Made, What They Aim At." Rome: Food and Agriculture Organization of the U.N.

———. 1953. *School Feeding: Its Contribution to Child Nutrition*. Rome: Food and Agriculture Organization of the U.N.

———. 1961a. "Ad-Hoc Advisory Committee on the Utilization of Food Surpluses, Summary Record of the Sixth Meeting." April 7. Rome: Food and Agriculture Organization of the U.N.

———. 1961b. "Ad-hoc Advisory Committee on the Utilization of Food Surpluses, Summary Record of Seventh Meeting." April 10. Rome: Food and Agriculture Organization of the U.N.

———. 1961c. "FAO/U.N. Proposal Regarding Procedures and Arrangements for Multilateral Utilization of Surplus Foods." November 4. Rome: Food and Agriculture Organization of the U.N.

———. 1962. "World Food Program, Summary Records." April 16 and 17. Rome: Food and Agriculture Organization of the U.N.

———. 1965a. *Food Aid and Education*. Rome: Food and Agriculture Organization of the U.N.

———. 1965b. *Operational and Administrative Problems of Food Aid*. Rome: Food and Agriculture Organization of the U.N.

———. 1965c. "Report on the World Food Program by the Executive Director." Rome: Food and Agriculture Organization of the U.N.

———. 2014. *The State of Food Insecurity in the World*. Rome: Food and Agriculture Organization of the U.N.

Federico, Giovanni. 2012. "Natura Non Fecit Saltus: The 1930s as the Discontinuity in the History of European Agriculture." In *War, Agriculture, and Food: Rural Europe from the 1930 to the 1950s,* edited by Paul Brassley, Yves Segers, and Leen Van Molle, 15–32. New York: Routledge.

Finkel, Alvin. 2006. *Social Policy and Practice in Canada: A History.* Ontario: Wilfred Laurier University Press.

Finnemore, Martha. 1996. "Norms, Culture, and World Politics: Insights from Sociology's Institutionalism." *International Organization* 50, no. 2: 325–47.

Finnemore, Martha, and Kathryn Sikkink. 1998. "International Norm Dynamics and Political Change." *International Organization* 52, no. 4: 887–917.

Fizbein, Ariel, Dena Ringold, and Santhosh Srinivasan. 2011. "Cash Transfers, Children, and the Crisis: Protecting Current and Future Investments." *Development Policy Review* 29, no. 5: 585–601.

Fiszbein, Ariel, Norbert Schady, Francisco H. G. Ferreira, Margaret Grosh, Nial Kelleher, Pedro Olinto, and Emmanuel Skoufias. 2009. "Conditional Cash Transfers. Reducing Present and Future Poverty." Washington, DC: World Bank.

Flaquer, Lluís. 2000. "Is There a Southern European Model of Family Policy?" In *Families and Family Policies in Europe: Comparative Perspectives,* edited by Astrid Pfenning and Thomas Bahle, 15–33. Frankfort: Peter Lang.

Gal, John. 2009. "Is there an Extended Family of Mediterranean Welfare States; or, Did Beveridge and Bismarck take a Mediterranean Cruise Together?" Paper prepared at the SPA Annual Conference, June 29–July 1.

Gauthier, Anne Helene. 1996. *The State and the Family: A Comparative Analysis of Family Policies in Industrialized Countries.* Oxford: Clarendon Press.

George, Alexander, and Andrew Bennett. 2005. *Case Studies and Theory Development in the Social Sciences.* Cambridge, MA: MIT Press.

Gerhard, Gesine. 2012. "Change in the European Countryside: Peasants and Democracy in Germany, 1935–1955" In *War, Agriculture, and Food: Rural Europe from the 1930 to the 1950s,* edited by Paul Brassley, Yves Segers, and Leen Van Molle, 195–208. New York: Routledge.

Gerschenkron, Alexander. 1962. *Economic Backwardness in Historical Perspective.* Cambridge, MA: Harvard University Press.

Gillard, Derek. 2003. "Food for Thought: Child Nutrition, the School Dinner, and the Food Industry." Accessed June 14, 2014. http://www.educationengland.org.uk/articles/22food.html.

Goldstein, Judith, and Robert O. Keohane. 1993. *Ideas and Foreign Policy: Beliefs, Institutions, and Political Change.* Ithaca, NY: Cornell University Press.

Gough, Ian, and Geof Wood with Armando Barrientos, Philippa Bevan, Peter Davis and Graham Room. 2004. *Insecurity and Welfare Regimes in Asia, Africa, and Latin America: Social Policy in Development Contexts.* Cambridge: Cambridge University Press.

Greenlagh, Trisha, Elizabeth Kristjansson, and Vivian Robinson. 2007. "Realist Review to Understand the Efficacy of School Feeding Programmes." *BMJ* 335: 858–61.

Grugel, Jean, and Pía Riggirozzi, eds. 2009. *Governance after Neoliberalism in Latin America*. New York: Palgrave Macmillan.

Gullberg, Eva. 2006. "Food for Future Citizens: School Meal Culture in Sweden." *Food, Culture, and Society* 9: 337–43.

Gunderson, Gordon. 1971. "The National School Lunch Program: Background and Development." Washington, DC: USDA.

Hagemann, Karen. 2011. "A Western German '*Sonderweg*'? Family, Work, and the Half-Day Time Policy of Childcare and Schooling." In *Children, Families, and the State: Time Policies of Childcare, Preschool, and Primary Education in Europe*, edited by Karen Hagemann, Konrad H. Jarausch, and Cristina Allemann-Ghionada, 275–300. New York: Berghahn Books.

Hagemann, Karen, Konrad H. Jarausch, and Cristina Allemann-Ghionada, eds. 2011. *Children, Families, and the State: Time Policies of Childcare, Preschool, and Primary Education in Europe*. New York: Berghahn Books.

Hall, Anthony. 2007. "Social Policies in the World Bank: Paradigms and Challenges." *Global Social Policy* 7: 151–75.

Hall, Stuart, Doreen Massey, and Michael Rustin. 2013. "After Neoliberalism: Analysing the Present." *Soundings: A Journal of Politics and Culture* 53: 8–22.

Handelman, Howard. 2009. *The Challenge of Third World Development*. 5th ed. Englewood, NJ: Prentice Hall.

Harman, Dana, 2008. "Rising Price of Rice Keeps U.N. Scrambling to Feed World's Hungry." *Christian Science Monitor*, May 21.

Harvey, David. 2005. *A Brief History of Neoliberalism*. Oxford: Oxford University Press.

Hatton, Timothy J., and Richard M. Martin. 2010. "The Effects on Stature of Poverty, Family Size, and Birth Order: British Children in the 1930s." *Oxford Economic Papers* 62, no. 1: 157–84.

Heclo, Hugh. 1974. *Modern Social Politics in Britain and Sweden*. New Haven: Yale University Press.

Hobson, Barbara, and Marika Lindholm. 1997. "Collective Identities, Women's Power Resources, and the Making of Welfare States." *Theory and Society* 26, no. 4: 475–508.

Hoffman, Florian, and Fernando Bentes. 2008. "Accountability for Social and Economic Rights in Brazil." In *Courting Social Justice: Judicial Enforcement of Social and Economic Rights in the Developing World*, edited by Varun Gauri and Daniel Brinks, 100–145. New York: Cambridge University Press.

Hopkins, Raymond, and Donald Puchala. 1978. *The Global Political Economy of Food*. Madison: University of Wisconsin Press.

House Committee on Agriculture. 1945. Hearings. March 23, 26–30, April 16–18, May 9–11, 22, 25.

House Committee on Agriculture. 1946. Report P.L. 396–79th Congress, June 4.

House Committee on Appropriations. 1945. Hearings. February 14, 26, 27, March 2, 3, 5–8.

House of Representatives. 1945. Report No. 684, June 5.

House of Representatives. 1946. Report No. 2080, May 20.

Huber, Evelyne, and John D. Stephens. 2001. *Development and Crisis of the Welfare State: Parties and Policies in Global Markets*. Chicago: University of Chicago Press.

Hyndman, B. 2000. "Feeding the Body, Feeding the Mind: An Overview of School-based Nutrition Programs in Canada." Breakfast for Learning Canadian Living Foundation.

International Food Policy Research Institute. 2004. "The Promise of School Feeding." Washington, DC: International Food Policy Research Institute.

Ismael, Shereen. 2006. *Child Poverty and the Canadian Welfare State: From Entitlement to Charity*. Alberta: University of Alberta Press.

Jackson, Peter. 2008. "U.N. Chronicle, Partnership for Development." Accessed October 15, 2010. http://www.un.org/Pubs/chronicle/2007/issue4/0407p07.html.

Jolly, Richard. 2010. "The U.N. and Development Policies." U.N. Intellectual History Project, Briefing Note Number 7.

Kääriäinen, Juha, and Heikki Lehtonen. 2006. "The Variety of Social Capital in Welfare State Regimes—a Comparative Study of 21 Countries." *European Societies* 8: 27–57.

Kahl, Colin H. 2006. *States, Scarcity, and Civil Strife in the Developing World*. Princeton, NJ: Princeton University Press.

Kanbur, Ravi. 2004. "The Development of Development Thinking." Lecture at the Institute for Social and Economic Change. Bangalore. June 10.

Katzenstein, Peter, ed. 1996. *The Culture of National Security: Norms and Identity in World Politics*. New York: Columbia University Press.

Keck, Margaret E., and Kathryn Sikkink. 1998. *Activists Beyond Borders: Advocacy Networks in International Politics*. Ithaca, NY: Cornell University Press.

Kenney, Sally J. 2003. "Where Is Gender in Agenda Setting." *Women and Politics* 25: 179–207.

Kingdon, John. 2003. *Agendas, Alternatives, and Public Policies*. 2nd ed. New York: Longman Press.

Kjaernes, U. 2003. "Experiences with the Norwegian Nutrition Policy." *Appetite* 41: 251–57.

Kneen, Brewster. 2002. *Invisible Giant: Cargill and Its Transnational Strategies*. London: Pluto Press.

Kohli, Atul. 2004. *State-Directed Development: Political Power and Industrialization in the Global Periphery*. Cambridge: Cambridge University Press.

Korpi, Walter. 1983. *The Democratic Class Struggle*. London: Routledge.

———. 1989. "Power, Politics, and State Autonomy in the Development of Social Citizenship." *American Sociological Review* 54, no. 3: 309–28.

Korsvold, Tora. 2011. "The Best Interest of the Child: Early Childhood Education in Norway and Sweden since 1945." In *Children, Families, and the State: Time Policies of Childcare, Preschool, and Primary Education in Europe*, edited by Karen

Hagemann, Konrad H. Jarausch, and Cristina Allemann-Ghionada, 137–55. New York: Berghahn Books.

Kunin, Madeline. 2012. *The New Feminist Agenda: Defining the Next Revolution for Women, Work and Family.* White River Junction, VT: Chelsea Green Publishing.

The Lancet. 1883. August 4.

Land, H., and R. Parker. 1978. "Family Policies in Britain: the Hidden Dimensions." In *Family Policy: Government and Families in Fourteen Countries,* edited by S. B. Kammerman and A. J. Kahn, 331–66. New York: Columbia University Press.

Lappe, Frances Moore, Joseph Collins, and Cary Fowler. 1977. *Food First: Beyond the Myth of Scarcity.* Boston: Houghton Mifflin.

Lavinas, Lena. 2013. "21st Century Welfare." *New Left Review* 84: 5–40.

Leach, Leisl. 1994. "PL 480 Food Aid: History and Legislation, Programs, and Policy Issues." CRS Report for Congress. Washington DC: Congressional Research Service.

Levine, Susan. 2008. *School Lunch Politics: The Surprising History of America's Favorite Welfare Program.* Princeton, NJ: Princeton University Press.

Lewis, Jane. 1992. "Gender and the Development of Welfare States." *Journal of European Social Policy* 2: 59–73.

Lewis, Timothy. 2007. *In the Long Run We're All Dead: The Canadian Turn to Fiscal Restraint.* Vancouver: UBC Press.

Lindert, Peter H. 1991. "Historical Patterns of Agricultural Policy." In *Agriculture and the State: Growth, Employment, and Poverty in Developing Countries,* edited by C. Peter Timmer, 29–83. Ithaca, NY: Cornell University Press.

Lipton, Michael. 1977. *Why Poor People Stay Poor: Urban Bias in World Development.* Cambridge, MA: Harvard University Press.

Locke, Richard M., and Kathleen Thelen. 1995. "Apples and Oranges Revisited: Contextualized Comparisons and the Study of Comparative Labor Politics." *Politics and Society* 23: 337–68.

Lomeli, Enrique Valancia. 2009. "Conditional Cash Transfer Programs: Achievements and Illusions." *Global Social Policy* 9: 167–71.

Lowi, Theodore J. 1972. "Four Systems of Policy, Politics, and Choice." *Public Administration Review* 32: 298–310.

Luhe, Eberhard. 1986. *The World Food Programme: 25 Years on Food Aid for Development and Emergencies.* Internal WFP Document.

Lundahl, Lisbeth. 2011. "The Scandinavian Model: The Time Policy of Primary School Education in Twentieth-Century Sweden." In *Children, Families, and the State: Time Policies of Childcare, Preschool, and Primary Education in Europe,* edited by Karen Hagemann, Konrad H. Jarausch, and Cristina Allemann-Ghionada, 156–74. New York: Berghahn Books.

Mahoney, James, and Gary Goertz. 2004. "The Possibility Principle: Choosing Negative Cases in Comparative Research." *American Political Science Review* 98: 653–69.

Mahoney, James, and Dietrich Rueschemeyer, eds. 2003. *Comparative Historical Analysis in the Social Sciences*. Cambridge: Cambridge University Press.

Maluccio, John A., and Rafael Flores. 2005. *Impact Evaluation of a Conditional Cash Transfer Program: The Nicaraguan Red de Protección Social*. Washington, DC: International Food Policy Research Institute.

Marshall, Dominique. 1999. "The Construction Children as an Object of International Relations: The Declaration of Children's Rights and the Child Welfare Committee of League of Nations, 1900–1924." *International Journal of Children's Rights* 7: 103–47.

Martiin, Carin. 2012. "Farming, Favoured in Times of Fear: Swedish Agricultural Policies, 1935–1955." In *War, Agriculture, and Food: Rural Europe from the 1930 to the 1950s*, edited by Paul Brassley, Yves Segers, and Leen Van Molle, 156–71. New York: Routledge.

Martin, John, and Ernst Langthaler. 2012. "Paths to Productivism: Agricultural Regulation in the Second World War and Its Aftermath in Great Britain and German-Annexed Austria." In *War, Agriculture, and Food: Rural Europe from the 1930 to the 1950s*, edited by Paul Brassley, Yves Segers, and Leen Van Molle, 55–74. New York: Routledge.

McDonough, J. E. 1997. *Interests, Ideas, and Deregulation*. Ann Arbor: University of Michigan Press.

McGovern, George. 1964. *War Against Want: America's Food for Peace Program*. New York: Walker and Company.

———. 2001. *The Third Freedom: Ending Hunger in Our Time*. New York: Simon and Schuster.

McLaughlin, Kathleen. 1943. "War-Nursery Needs: Care of Children of Working Mothers Presents Some Baffling Problems" *New York Times,* February 21.

Mehrotra, Santosh. 1998. "Education for All: Policy Lessons from High-Achieving Countries." *International Review of Education* 44: 461–84.

Menzies, Merril W. 1973. "Grain Marketing Methods in Canada—the Theory, Assumptions, and Approach." *American Journal of Agricultural Economics* 55: 791–99.

Mettler, Suzanne. 1998. *Dividing Citizens: Gender and Federalism in New Deal Public Policy*. Ithaca, NY: Cornell University Press.

———. 2005. *Soldiers to Citizens: The GI Bill and the Making of the Greatest Generation*. New York: Oxford University Press.

Miller del Rosso, Joyce. 1999. "School Feeding Programs: Improving Effectiveness and Increasing the Benefit to Education. A Guide for Program Managers." Washington, DC: Partnership for Child Development.

Miner, William A., and Dale E. Hathaway. 1988. *World Agricultural Trade: Building a Consensus*. Washington DC: Peterson Institute.

Mink, Gwendolyn. 1994. "Welfare Reform in Historical Perspective" *Social Justice* 21, no. 1: 114–31.

Ministry of Information. 1946. *How Britain Was Fed in Wartime, 1939–45,* London: HMSO.

Minneapolis Star Tribune. 2004. "Q&A: George McGovern: Maybe for the First Time in Human History We Can Resolve World Hunger." November 21.

Mission: Readiness. 2010. Too Fat to Fight. Accessed April 23, 2014. http://cdn.mis-sionreadiness.org/MR_Too_Fat_to_Fight-1.pdf.

Mitchell, Jonathan, and Henri Leturque. 2011. "WFP 2008–2013 Purchase for Progress (P4P). Initiative: A Strategic Evaluation (mid-term)." Rome: World Food Programme.

Molyneux, Maxine. 2006. "Mothers at the Service of the New Poverty Agenda: Progresa/Oportunidades, Mexico's Conditional Cash Transfer Programme." *Social Policy and Administratio* 40, no. 4: 425–49.

———. 2008. "Conditional Cash Transfers: A 'Pathway to Women's Empowerment'?" Pathways to Women's Empowerment Working Paper 5, Institute of Development Studies, Brighton.

Molyneux, Maxine, and Marilyn Thomson, 2011. "CCT Programmes and Women's Empowerment in Peru, Bolivia and Ecuador." CARE Policy Paper.

Morgan, Kimberly J. 2006. *Working Mothers and the Welfare State: Religion and the Politics of Work-Family Policies in Western Europe and the United States.* Stanford, CA: Stanford University Press.

Mousseau, Frederic. 2005. "Food Aid and Food Sovereignty: Ending World Hunger in Our Time." Oakland Institute.

Myrdal, Alva, and Gunnar Myrdal. 1934. *Crisis in the Population Question.* Stockholm: Bonniers.

Naldini, Manuela. 2003. *The Family in the Mediterranean Welfare States.* New York: Routledge.

NEPAD. 2001. "The New Partnership for Africa's Development." Abuja, Nigeria: NEPAD.

NEPAD Secretariat. 2002. "Implementing the Comprehensive Africa Agriculture Development Programme and Resorting Food Security in Africa: The Roadmap." Midrand, South Africa: NEPAD.

New York Times. 1913. "School Lunch Problem, Solved, Now Strikes a Snag." January 12.

———. 1918a. "Underfed Children, Grave City Problem." January 13.

———. 1918b. "School Luncheons Before Aldermen." February 15.

———. 1918c. "May Favor School Lunch." March 6.

———. 1918d. "Plea for School Lunches." August 9.

———. 1927. "School Lunches Are Called Unfit." October 31.

———. 1932. "School Relief Fund Faces Wider Need." January 31.

———. 1939. "5,000,000 Pupils to Get Free Lunches from FSCC in Use of Farm Surpluses." August 23.

———. 1943a. "School Lunches Put Up to Mayor." June 16.

———. 1943b. "School Lunches Saved: Milk Program Covered." July 10.

———. 1944. "School Lunch Plan Urged on Senators." May 5.

———. 1946. "Truman Approves School Lunch Bill." June 5.

Nussbaum, Martha. 1992. "Human Functioning and Social Justice: In Defense of Aristotelian Essentialism." *Political Theory* 20, no. 2: 202–46.

———. 2000. *Women and Human Development: The Capabilities Approach.* Cambridge: Cambridge University Press.

O'Connor, Julia S. 1996. "From Women in the Welfare State to Gendering Welfare State Regimes." *Current Sociology* 44, no. 2: 1–130.

O'Connor, Julia S., Ann Shola Orloff, and Sheila Shaver. 1999. *States, Markets, Families: Gender, Liberalism, and Social Policy in Australia, Canada, Great Britain, and the United States.* Cambridge: Cambridge University Press.

OECD. 2013. "Employment Rate of Women." Employment and Labour Markets: Key Tables from OECD No. 5.

Ohlander, Ann-Sofie. 1991. "The Invisible Child? The Struggle for a Social Democratic Family Policy in Sweden, 1900–1960s." In *Maternity and Gender Policies: Women and the Rise of the European Welfare States, 1880s–1950s,* edited by Gisela Bock and Pat Thane, 60–72. New York: Routledge.

Olson, Mancur. 1965 (2003). *The Logic of Collective Action: Public Goods and the Theory of Groups.* Cambridge, MA: Harvard University Press.

Opppenheim, Beatrice. 1943. "More School Lunches." *New York Times,* September 26.

Osowoski, Christine Persson. 2012. "The Swedish School Meal as a Public Meal: Collective Thinking, Actions, and Meal Patterns." PhD diss., Uppsala University.

Owusu, Francis. 2003. "Pragmatism and the Gradual Shift from Dependency to Neoliberalism: The World Bank, African Leaders, and Development Policy in Africa." *World Development* 31: 1655–72.

Passmore, S., and G. Harris. 2004. "School Nutrition Actions Groups and Their Effects on Secondary Aged Children's Food Choices." *British Nutrition Foundation, Nutrition Bulletin* 30: 364–69.

Pero, Valeria, and Dimitri Szerman. 2010. "The New Generation of Social Programs in Brazil." In *Conditional Cash Transfers in Latin America,* edited by Mitchell Adato and John Hoddinott, 78–100. Baltimore: John Hopkins University Press.

Pierson, Paul. 1994. *Dismantling the Welfare State?: Reagan, Thatcher and the Politics of Retrenchment.* Cambridge: Cambridge University Press.

———. 2000. "Increasing Returns, Path Dependence, and the Study of Politics." *American Political Science Review* 94, no. 2: 251–67.

———. 2004. *Politics in Time: History, Institutions, and Social Analysis.* Princeton, NJ: Princeton University Press.

Pildes, Richard H. 1991. "The Unintended Cultural Consequences of Public Policy: A Comment on the Symposium." *Michigan Law Review* 89, no. 4: 936–78.

Rapley, John. 2007. *Understanding Development: Theory and Practice in the Third World.* 3rd ed. Boulder, CO: Lynne Reinner.

Risse-Kappen, Thomas, Stephen C. Roop, and Kathryn Sikkink. eds. 1999. *The Power of Human Rights: International Norms and Domestic Change*. New York: Cambridge University Press.

Rothermund, Dietmar. 1996. *The Global Impact of the Great Depression: 1929–1939*. New York: Routledge.

Rowntree, Benjamin Seebohm. 1941. *Poverty and Progress: A Second Social Survey of York*. London: Longmans, Green.

Rutledge, Jennifer Geist. 2012. "Courts as Entrepreneurs: The Case of the Indian Mid-Day Meals Programme." *Asian Politics and Policy* 4, no. 4: 527–47.

Ruttan, Vernon W. 1993. *Why Food Aid?* Baltimore: John Hopkins University Press.

Sainsbury, Diane, ed. 1999. *Gender and Welfare State Regimes*. New York: Oxford University Press.

Scott, Marjorie. 1953. *School Feeding: Its Contribution to Child Nutrition*. Rome: Food and Agriculture Organizations of the United Nations.

Seip, Anne-Lise, and Hilde Ibsen. 1991. "Family Welfare, Which policy? Norway's Road to Child Allowances." In *Maternity and Gender Policies: Women and the Rise of the European Welfare States, 1880s–1950s*, edited by Gisela Bock and Pat Thane, 40–59. New York: Routledge.

Sejersted, Francis. 2011. *The Age of Social Democracy: Norway and Sweden in the Twentieth Century*. Princeton, NJ: Princeton University Press.

Sen, Amartya. 1999. *Development as Freedom*. New York: Alfred A. Knopf.

Sen, B. R. 1982. *Towards a Newer World: The Life of a Senior Indian Diplomat and Former Director-General of the Food and Agriculture Organization of the United Nations*. Dublin: Tycooly International Publishing.

Shaw, D. John. 2001. *The U.N. World Food Programme and the Development of Food Aid*. New York: Palgrave.

———. 2007. *World Food Security: A History Since 1945*. New York: Palgrave.

Sheingate, Adam D. 2003. *The Rise of the Agricultural Welfare State: Institutions and Interest Group Power in the United States, France, and Japan*. Princeton, NJ: Princeton University Press.

Short, Brian. 2012. "The Social Impact of State Control of Agriculture in Britain, 1939–1955." In *War, Agriculture, and Food: Rural Europe from the 1930 to the 1950s*, edited by Paul Brassley, Yves Segers, and Leen Van Molle, 172–93. New York: Routledge.

Sikkink, K. 1991. *Ideas and Institutions: Developmentalism in Brazil and Argentina*. Ithaca: Cornell University Press.

Simon-Kumar, Rachel. 2011. "The Analytics of 'Gendering' the Post-neoliberal State." *Social Politics* 18: 441–68.

Singer, Hans, John Wood, and Tony Jennings. 1987. *Food Aid: The Challenge and the Opportunity*. Oxford: Clarendon Press.

Skidmore, Thomas, and Peter Smith. 1997. *Modern Latin America*. 4th ed. Oxford: Oxford University Press.

Skocpol, Theda. 1979. *States and Social Revolutions: A Comparative Analysis of France, Russia, and China*. Cambridge: Cambridge University Press.

———. 1992. *Protecting Soldiers and Mothers*. Cambridge, MA: Belknap Press of Harvard University Press.

———. 2003. "Doubly Engaged Social Science: The Promise of Comparative Historical Analysis." In *Comparative Historical Analysis in the Social Sciences*, edited by James Mahoney and Dietrich Rueschemeyer, 407–428. New York: Cambridge University Press.

Smedley, Emma. 1930. *The School Lunch: Its Organization and Management in Philadelphia*. Pennsylvania: Emma Smedley.

Smith, Matthew. 2012. *Hyperactive: The Controversial History of ADHD*. London: Reaktion Books.

Sörensen, Kerstin. 2011. "Party Platforms and Public Childcare: Structural and Ideational Factors Shaping Policy in Norway and Sweden." *Scandinavian Political Studies* 34, no. 1: 1–26.

Sörensen, Kerstin, and Christina Bergqvist. 2002. *Gender and the Social Democratic Welfare Regime: A Comparison of Gender-Equality-Friendly Policies in Sweden and Norway*. National Institute for Working Life (Arbetslivsinstitutet).

Soss, Joe. 1999. "Lessons of Welfare: Policy Design, Political Learning, and Political Action." *American Political Science Review* 93, no. 2: 363–80.

Spargo, John. 1906. *The Bitter Cry of the Children*. New York: Macmillan.

Starke, Peter. 2006. "The Politics of Welfare State Retrenchment: A Literature Review." *Social Policy and Administration* 40, no. 1: 104–20.

Starr Center Association of Philadelphia, Records 1894–1973. Accessed July 13, 2011. http://www.nursing.upenn.edu/history/Documents/Starr%20Centre%20Association%200f%20Philadelphia.pdf.

Stephens, John D. 1979. *The Transition from Capitalism to Socialism*. London: Macmillan.

Stiglitz, Joseph. 2002. "Development Policies in a World of Globalization." Paper presented at New International Trends for Economic Development seminar, Rio de Janiero, Brazil. September 12–13.

Stone, Deborah A. 1989. "Causal Stories and the Formation of Policy Agendas." *Political Science Quarterly* 104, no. 2: 281–300.

Stortingsforhandlinger (Proceedings of Parliament). 1945–46, vol. 8.

Strach, Patricia. 2007. *All in the Family: The Private Roots of American Public Policy*. Stanford, CA: Stanford University Press.

Suchman, M. C. 1997. "On Beyond Interest: Rational, Normative, and Cognitive Perspectives in the Social Scientific Study of Law." *Wisconsin Law Review* 3: 475–501.

Sugiyama, Natasha Borges. 2008. "Ideology and Social Networks: The Politics of Social Policy Diffusion in Brazil." PhD diss., University of Texas at Austin.

Thelen, Kathleen. 1999. "Historical Institutionalism in Comparative Politics." *Annual Review of Political Science* 2: 369–404.

The Times [London]. 1905. "Hungry School Children." January 6.

———. 1937. "Free Meals in Schools." February 4.

———. 1941a. "Food to See U.S. Through." August 11.

———. 1941b. "The Children's Share: School Meals in War-Time: A Social Necessity." September 22.

———. 1941c. "Mid-Day Meals in All Schools." October 1.

———. 1941d. "Letter to the Editor: School Meals." October 1.

———. 1941e. "School Meals: The Needs of the Child." October 11.

———. 1943. "National Health in War-Time." June 16.

Titmuss, R. M. 1958. *Essays on the Welfare State.* London: Allen and Unwin.

Tomlinson, Mark. 2007. "School Feeding in East and Southern Africa: Improving Food Sovereignty or Photo Opportunity?" Equinet Discussion Paper Number 46, March.

UNCTAD Document. 2008. The High Level Conference on World Food Security. May 30.

Ungerson, Clare, and Mary Kember. 1997. *Women and Social Policy: A Reader.* 2nd ed. New York: Palgrave Macmillan.

U.N. 1960. General Assembly Resolution No. 1496 (XV), October 27.

———. 2008. "The U.N. System Response to the World Food Security Crisis." New York: Food Crisis Center.

U.N. Millennium Project Task Force on Hunger. 2005. *Halving Hunger: It Can Be Done.* London: Earthscan.

U.S. Department of Agriculture. 1957. *Agricultural Policies of Foreign Governments Including Trade Policies Affecting Agriculture.* Agricultural Handbook No. 132.

U.S. Senate. 1945. Report 553, July 28.

———. 1956. Hearings on Senate Resolution 85 and S. 86. May 28.

———. 1959. Senate Report No. 1922, August 24.

U.S. Senate. Committee on Agriculture and Forestry. 1944. Hearings, May 2–5.

U.S. Senate. Foreign Relations Committee. 1959. Senate Bill 1711.

Valdes, Alberto. 1991. "The Role of Agricultural Exports in Development." In *Agriculture and the State: Growth, Employment, and Poverty in Developing Countries,* edited by C. Peter Timmer, 84–115. Ithaca, NY: Cornell University Press.

Van Evera, Stephen. 1997. *Guide to Methods for Students of Political Science.* Ithaca, NY: Cornell University Press.

Vernon, James. 2007. *Hunger.* Cambridge, MA: Harvard University Press.

Vetterlein, Antje. 2007. "Economic Growth, Poverty Reduction, and the Role of Social Policies: The Evolution of the World Bank's Social Development Approach." *Global Governance* 13: 513–33.

Village Hope. 2008. "School Feeding Programs: Summary of the Literature and Best Practices" Boise, ID: Village Hope.

Way, Wendy. 2013. *A New Idea Each Morning: How Food and Agriculture Came Together in One International Organization.* Canberra: Australian National University E Press.

Weber, Max. 1946. *From Max Weber: Essays in Sociology*. Edited and translated by H. H. Gerth and C. Wright Mills. New York: Oxford University Press.

Webster, Charles. 1993. *Caring for Health: History and Diversity*. Buckingham: Open University Press.

Weinreb, Alice. 2011. "Matters of Taste: The Politics of Food in Divided Germany, 1945–1971." *Bulletin of the GHI*.

———. 2012. "'For the Hungry Have No Past nor Do They Belong to a Political Party': Debates over German Hunger after World War II." *Central European History* 45, no. 1: 50–78.

Weisfeld-Adams, Emma, and Anastasia Andrzejewski. 2008. "Hunger and Poverty: Definitions and Distinction." The Hunger Project.

White, Ann Folino. 2015. *Plowed Under: Food Policy Protests and Performance in New Deal America*. Bloomington: Indiana University Press.

Wibberley, John. 2008. "A Brief History of Agriculture in the UK." RuSource: Briefing 193.

Winders, Bill. 2009. *The Politics of Food Supply: U.S. Agricultural Policy in the World Economy*. New Haven: Yale University Press.

World Food Programme. 2006. "World Hunger Series 2006: Hunger and Learning." Rome: World Food Programme.

———. 2007. Support to NEPAD Report. Period of Report: July 2006 – June 2007. Rome.

———. 2011a. "Agricultural Learning and Impacts Network (ALINe): P4P Global Gender Strategy." Rome: World Food Programme.

———. 2011b. "Agricultural Learning and Impacts Network (ALINe): P4P and Gender: Literature Review and Fieldwork Report." Rome: World Food Programme.

———. 2013. "State of School Feeding." Rome: World Food Programme.

———. 2014a. "About." Rome: World Food Programme.

———. 2014b. "Two Minutes to Learn About: School Meals." Rome: World Food Programme.

Yaschine, Iliana. 1998. "The Changing Anti-poverty Agenda: What Can the Mexican Case Tell Us?" MPhil. thesis, University of Sussex.

Yaschine, Iliana, and Monica E. Orozco. 2010. "The Evolving Antipoverty Agenda in Mexico: The Political Economy of PROGRESA and Oportunidades." In *Conditional Cash Transfers in Latin America*, edited by Mitchell Adato and John Hoddinott, 55–77. Baltimore: John Hopkins University Press.

Yates, Julian S., and Karen Bakker. 2014. "Debating the 'Post-neoliberal Turn' in Latin America." *Progress in Human Geography* 38, no. 1: 62–90.

Zelizer, Vivian. 1985. *Pricing the Priceless Child: The Changing Social Value of Children*. New York: Basic Books.

Zuckerman, Michael. 2003. "Epilogue: The Millennium of Childhood That Stretches Before Us." In *Beyond the Century of the Child*, edited by Willem Koops and Michael Zuckerman, 225–42. Philadelphia: University of Pennsylvania Press.

INDEX

ABOUT THE AUTHOR

JENNIFER GEIST RUTLEDGE received her PhD from the University of Minnesota and is currently an assistant professor of political science at John Jay College. Her work focuses on food politics within the context of public policy and comparative politics, and she has published articles in journals such as *Food Culture and Society, Asian Politics and Policy,* and *History of Education.*

CPSIA information can be obtained
at www.ICGtesting.com
Printed in the USA
BVOW11s0214090416
443451BV00006B/16/P